WRITTEN SPECIFICALLY FOR MIDDLE INCOME PEOPLE!

ORGANIZATION AND EFFICIENCY IN PERSONAL FINANCES

RUZANNA KRDILYAN HERNANDEZ, ED.D.

Higher Ground Books & Media
Springfield, Ohio.
http://highergroundbooksandmedia.com

Printed in the United States of America 2021

WRITTEN SPECIFICALLY FOR MIDDLE INCOME PEOPLE!

ORGANIZATION AND EFFICIENCY IN PERSONAL FINANCES

RUZANNA KRDILYAN HERNANDEZ, ED.D.

Table of Contents

Chapter 1
Introduction

The Struggle with Money and Personal Finances

Right after I finished college, I started my own small business. A new client, a man in his mid-thirties, called me to ask me if I could help him. He said he saw the word "financial" in the title of my business and thought I could assist. He was financially broke and could not figure out what to do – he did not know how to get out of the situation, and even worse, he did not know how he even got to that point. He explained that he had a job, making a decent middle-income salary. He was married with four children, and his wife was not working to stay home and care for the children. This nice man said he would pay for my time if I could look at his finances and see how I could help.

My bachelor's degree was in Finance, and I worked in the financial, accounting, and insurance sectors since the age of 17. I learned more about money and money management during those years at California State University than I had ever learned growing up. Part of my office operations involved helping people who were in the lower, middle, or upper-middle-income levels handle their tax situations, insurance, and personal finances.

I met with this client in person a few days later. The bottom line was this: He knew how much money was coming in because it was fixed income from his job. However, he had no idea how much in debt he was, how much was going toward food each month, gasoline, insurance, etc. He was racking up debt and being hustled by creditors because he was falling increasingly into the abyss. The money spent was far outweighing the money earned. Ultimately, he realized he had to file for bankruptcy and get organized with his spending. He also admitted he needed to generate more income to sustain his lifestyle or make significant changes.

Throughout my life, I have met hundreds of people who have similar situations, just like this particular client. They are devastated by their money problems even though they make a decent income! My observations and research have pointed to a few compelling commonalities throughout their stories.

Explanation of Middle-Class Income

What we consider middle-class income really depends on where a person lives. A person can make $65,000 and live comfortably in a more rural area than he or she would in a metropolitan area, like New York or Los Angeles. Some places have a very high cost of living, while other locations do not. According to Worldpopulationreview.com, Hawaii is ranked as the state with the highest median rent at $1,617, whereas West Virginia has the same home rent for a median price of $725.

Figure 1: Average Rent Per State

State	Average Rent (median)
Hawaii	$1,617
California	$1,503
New York	$1,280
Florida	$1,175
Texas	$1,045
Illinois	$1,010
Georgia	$1,006
Pennsylvania	$938
Ohio	$808
West Virginia	$725

https://worldpopulationreview.com/state-rankings/average-rent-by-state

If we judge based solely on median rental values, it is obvious where the cost of living is more and where it is less. However, other factors play a part, also. Gasoline costs, food costs, insurance costs, etcetera, all play a role in how the cost of living is calculated. City by city, there is a difference in median rents. San Francisco's median rent is $3,500, according to 2018 data for a 1-bedroom apartment (Fortunebuilders.com). Within each state, there could be a massive difference in the cost of living, depending on the city of residence. In the state of California, this is what one would expect to pay, on average, for rent. A person living in the same home in San Francisco will pay about three times more than in Victorville.

As it is obvious, $65,000 of income for one person can go a long way if a person is living in a state like Arkansas, or West Virginia, versus New York or Hawaii. According to USNews.com, low income is considered an income of less than $40,100 for a family of three, according to 2018 data. Middle income is $40,100 to $120,400, and upper income is over $120,400. A breakdown of income class, using 2019 data, for a family of three, is broken down like this:

Figure 2: Breakdown of Income Classes

Income Group	Income
Poor or nearly poor	At or below $32,048
Lower-middle class	$32,048 - $53,413
Middle class	$53,413 - $106,827
Upper-middle class	$106,827 - $373,894
Rich	Over $373,894

Let's keep in mind that this is income information only and does not consider the cost of living. The data is for a family of three individuals. A family of five individuals will have a harder time managing a budget with an income of $55,000, for example, than a family of three.

It's also important to note that it's not easy to move to an area where the costs are lower because, generally speaking, that's not where one finds higher-paying jobs. Jobs are plentiful in more urban and metropolitan areas, even though the cost of living is higher. For example, there are plenty of people who work in New York City but cannot live in New York City due to the extremely high cost of living. They tend to move to the city's outskirts, or even in New Jersey, and just deal with the longer commute to afford a decent lifestyle. Sometimes people stay in more expensive areas out of necessity.

Financial struggles are real for many individuals and families, especially those in the middle- and lower-income levels. They exist because of various reasons. According to CBSnews.com, there are seven traits of people who struggle financially:

1) Income is volatile (changes every month)

2) They do not receive employee benefits

3) They have school-aged children

4) There are no financial plans, especially ahead of 5 years

5) They pay more than 30% of their income on rent or mortgage

6) They were never taught how to manage money by their parents

7) People are not confident about how to properly manage their money

Do any of these traits describe you? They have certainly described me at varying points of my life!

The idea is to learn ways to overcome financial challenges and to live a more financially sound life. This book has help, resources, and insights to make that happen for the reader. The focus is primarily on item #7 of the list. We can all become more confident in handling our finances with the information and resources.

Causes and Reasons for Poor Money Management

Before providing a step-by-step guide on personal money management, it is important to delve a bit more deeply into why people are not confident or knowledgeable about their money. These include:

- Hatred of math and having to calculate or budget

- State of confusion

- Overindulgence

- Overly hopeful attitude

- Depression and stress

There are other reasons for poor money management. One of these is a lack of budgeting which involves organization and planning. By learning better money management skills, people become more confident in how they save, spend, and invest for their future. Let's discuss each in more detail.

Hatred of Math – Even Simple Math

Because money involves adding and subtracting numbers in the hundreds and thousands, often involving decimals, people avoid dealing with it and managing it. This may be hard to believe, but it is true. Some people do not want to take the time to sit and count money to figure out what's coming in and what's going out. They want to avoid the math of budgeting as much as humanly possible. If I asked most clients what their most considerable expense was, they would undoubtedly say either their monthly rent or mortgage. What are the second and third largest expenses? That's another question. They might have an idea but not know exactly. Is their second most considerable monthly expense the telephone bill? Is it transportation? Is it food? What percentage of the total monthly income is food? What part of the total income is the cost of fun, recreation, and hobbies? To know would involve adding, subtracting, and organizing.

By taking baby steps, we can overcome the confusion and struggle with understanding basic math and use it to our advantage. We do not have to start calculating percentages right away. The goal is to overcome the hatred of math by doing some simple calculations once a week, preferably on the computer or using a calculator. Once we overcome the fear of using math, we can develop a personal budget and get on track with spending and saving goals.

"A budget is telling your money where to go instead of wondering where it went." -Dave Ramsey

State of Confusion

Being middle-class or in a middle-income household can be tricky. I am in the middle class now, but that was not the case when I was growing up. There were many things I could not afford to get when I was younger. Our total household income was below the poverty line.

I know I can afford nicer things now than I did when I was poor. However, like thousands of Americans, I overindulge. I convince myself that I can afford more than what I can. Take toothpaste as an example. I used to ONLY go to the dollar store to purchase toothpaste. As my income grew over the years, I decided that it was more convenient to buy the product from a grocery store (more expensive) and because I wanted better quality. The problem wasn't just toothpaste. I stopped buying many other things from the bargain stores. Spending on goods, products, and services was shifting because my income was increasing, but not proportionally. I was rewarding myself for earning more because I worked hard to get the education, skills, and expertise necessary to grow my income. However, I was overspending. Here is an illustration to explain my point:

Figure 3: Toothpaste example

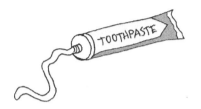   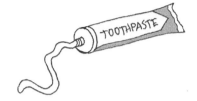

Purchase price $1.00   *Purchase price: $5.65*

Income: $30,500 per year   *Income: $48,000 per year*

Consider the example above. Technically, my new toothpaste purchase price should be about $1.60 with my increased income. What am I doing wrong, though? I am paying more than five times the price because I overestimate my buying power! Does this sound like you?

When people live in poverty, they don't even think to go near the malls and expensive grocery stores. They know what they can afford – they stick to the bare necessities and purchase from places that will help them survive from one day to the next.

People living in the upper class can afford all kinds of luxuries, so money on household goods is not an object. They can afford to splurge and can afford to buy impulsively.

People in the middle tend to be confused. People like me, who are in the "middle," know we can afford more but often overindulge and overthink how much more. We ask ourselves in a confused state at the stores, "Can I afford this at this price?" More often than not, the answer is we can't because we are making more money than before, but not enough to afford the higher-priced goods, at least not quite yet being in the middle-income arena.

15

Overindulgence

When people grow up in poverty, especially during their youth, they tend to feel deprived, especially if surrounded by others with overpriced sneakers, Michael Kors backpacks, and expensive jewelry. Those motivated and want more in life get out of poverty by working hard, getting an education, and realizing their goals and dreams. The American Dream is based on that creed: If you work hard and take advantage of opportunities that present themselves to you, you can become successful and thrive (Merriam-Webster, 2022). I am an example of a person who believed in this creed and took advantage of it. I grew up in poverty. I decided to pursue higher education and attend college. The road to success was difficult, but, like many others, I began a fantastic career in education after I finished college. My job led me to a more sound financial status.

People who find themselves out of poverty may feel like they have stronger buying power. They do, but they may tend to overindulge. Since they did not have luxuries in the past, they want to make up for that in their current state, even if they can't afford it all. I was one of those people. In my early twenties, I made decent money as an office manager but was living at home. My living expenses were low. I bought all kinds of things I could not afford and got into quite a bit of credit card debt. I paid it all off, but it took me years and quite a bit of stress to get out of the financial mess.

My story is not an exception. Overindulgence and debt are common for many young people who grow up in poverty. They get into major debt because they can't afford the luxuries they want.

Overly Hopeful Attitude

In the United States, we are used to purchasing things using credit cards. It's part of our lifestyle! We are accustomed to make a purchase now, like an expensive car, a bigger-than-necessary house, or luxurious furniture pieces because we assume the money will be there later to help us pay for these items. Millions of us have an overly hopeful attitude that money will come – it will be there to help pay for today's expenses.

I am also guilty of making indulgent purchases with high hopes that I can repay the debt later. In my early twenties, I started working in an office setting. I was so hopeful that my income would keep growing and growing. I decided to purchase expensive clothes, thinking they would help me feel more confident about myself. Of course, I was buying way more than I could afford. I knew this but chose to continue to purchase because I was *hopeful* that my income would somehow grow and I would pay off the debts I was incurring. I was young, and I figured as long as I was in college and on track to graduate, I would automatically get a better job with more pay. I could pay off the debt then!

I was naïve. I didn't realize that I would not "automatically" get more income after finishing school. My income did not grow as quickly as I had hoped. The situation left me in more debt than I wanted to be at a young age. Do you also have credit card debt? Did you accrue it by buying things you could not readily afford?

"Emotional shopping causes overspending. Reason out your purchases." -Maria James, the Money Specialist

People make all kinds of larger-than-necessary expenses, hoping they will pay for them later. This notion is especially the case with people who do not have a steady income each month, like self-employed individuals. Business owners often overthink how much money they will generate in the following month, so they tend to buy now in hopes of paying later. The "later" part takes years and costs more in interest.

"Life is too short."

Like people who are hopeful about their current purchases and future earnings, some develop a habit of buying even when they can't afford to because they perceive that life is too short. Thus, they overspend and develop a bad habit. They figure if they don't buy now, they will die tomorrow, having never enjoyed the finer things in life.

When we become more responsible with money, our mindset changes. For example, I often spent money wastefully on food in expensive restaurants. I told myself, "If I die tomorrow, at least I would feel happy knowing I ate a $60-plate of steak." Instead of being hopeful and cautious, I overspent, causing more stress than was necessary for myself in the days to come. I became more organized with my finances over time, which helped me kick the bad habit of overspending.

Depression and Stress

Feelings of depression and stress affect spending habits. Research shows people who are depressed tend to spend more than they can afford. They buy food from restaurants instead of cooking at home because of the stress and anxiety over having to prepare food. They don't have the energy to pay their bills, so they let them accumulate until they bring themselves to pay. The inability to pay on time results in additional fees. They can avoid the fees with proper money management (Thesimpledollar.com, 2021).

Stress causes overspending on items like food, clothing, and leisurely items. It leads to more debt, feelings of shame and agitation, and even low self-esteem. It may lead to compulsive spending and buying, which makes the problems even worse (Psychologytoday.com, 2021).

Compulsive spending during periods of high stress, anxiety, and depression could cripple a person financially and emotionally. According to a study by Northwestern Mutual, money is the number one source of stress for most American Adults (Huffpost.com, 2021). Stress and depression cause money disorder. Money disorder causes more stress and depression. It's a cycle that is difficult to break.

Figure 4: Cycle of Compulsive Spending

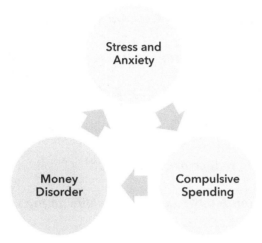

Knowing that this is a real condition that must be dealt with can lead to better money management, less stress, and more relief. Developing an organized way to manage money and understanding some of the poor spending habits will help lead to a better financial future.

Strategies, Ideas, and Steps to Improving Personal Finances

Based on what has been shared so far in this chapter, here are some strategies and ideas to help keep us all on track with better money management. Chapter 9 has a cumulation of all the actions and steps compiled in one place from all chapters.

Here are strategies and steps to follow to address some of the issues with overspending and under-saving based on this introductory chapter:

- *Write a goal to organize finances immediately. Here is an example: I will start using a monthly system to know exactly how much I am earning and how much I can afford to spend.*

- *Take about two hours to sit down and log into my checking account online.*

- *If the amount of money spent (going out) is more than the amount earned (coming in), focus on two things:*

  - *How can you generate more money? Can you get a promotion? Can you improve your skills to get a promotion? Can you start a side business that will generate more income immediately? Can you change jobs?*

  - *How can you spend less money? Can you take each item on my spending list and see if there is a way to reduce or eliminate it?*

- *Calendar a time each week or month to sit down (preferably on the weekend) for a 2-hour or 3-hour period to calculate money coming in and money going out (personal budget.*

- *Figure out which calculator you like the most; either the computer calculator, a phone, or an actual calculator purchased from an office supply store.*

- *Based on some reasons why people have difficulty with personal money management listed in chapter 1, pick which one(s) resonate(s) with me, if any. Figuring out the root cause will help me determine what you need to work on fixing.*

Conclusion

I wrote this book to help people struggling with personal financial management. The financial hardships I experienced in my twenties and early thirties were due to two main reasons: lack of knowledge and lack of organization with personal finances. Throughout my lifetime, I met many others with very similar situations. I hope the ideas and strategies I describe that have helped me become organized and efficient with money will resonate with readers and help them in their journey. Financial organization leads to saving more, spending less, having less stress, and feeling better about oneself, knowing that financial goals can easily be met.

Chapter 2
My Financial Struggles and What I Learned from Them

Money Management at a Young Age

Teaching kids money management is crucial to their financial health in the future. The idea of budgeting, setting limits, being disciplined with money and spending, and saving, are all very important life lessons that kids can learn once they are at an age where they start to understand that money is a precious commodity.

Most parents do not talk to their kids about specific financial issues and managing money. They figure their kids are too immature to understand spending and saving. For example, to a 10-year-old, spending money on games, amusement parks, and junk food is more important than a mortgage payment. They take for granted that the home they live in is there because someone is making monthly payments for it. They do not quite grasp the idea of installment payments until they become teenagers.

How much parents discuss finances with their kids is up to their comfort levels; however, financial talk must take some shape or form. Talking to them does not mean, "We don't have enough," and ending it. Talking means explaining, showing, giving causes and effects, etc. In other words, it involves getting kids to think critically about money as a necessity and a scarcity. Perhaps using examples, using references, stories, and anecdotes would help. The sooner parents introduce the following ideas to their kids, the better:

- How much is coming in must equal how much is going out

- Saving for "rainy days"

- Planning for the future (financially)

- Proper budgeting each month

- Spending on needs versus spending on desires

- How payment installments work

Personal Financial Struggles

Growing up, I often felt bad for my parents' financial struggles and wished I could help more. As a child, I did not know we were poor because everyone in my realm was also poor. In the Soviet Union, where my family came from initially, most people lived meager lives. A majority of middle-class people in the United States would not believe how people survived on so extraordinarily little under the Soviet socialist-communist system.

I was nine years old when my family and I moved out of Armenia in search of a better life in the U.S. In elementary school, reality set in. I quickly understood where my family stood financially compared to other school kids. Their clothes were better than mine. They brought money for lunch daily instead of free lunch; they had nicer pencil boxes than I did, etc. For the first time, I understood some people had very little money to make ends meet. At the same time, others had more and were comfortable financially. Income inequality was very apparent to me.

Since my mom was home taking care of my siblings and me, my dad did the heavy lifting when it came to working and bringing home money. He was the wage earner. His level of stress and anxiety was remarkable. He and my mom did everything they could to make ends meet. The problem was this: There was just enough each week to pay for food and rent. There was nearly nothing left, though, for extras and emergencies. It was very tough for them to put money aside.

Immigrant families are almost twice as likely to be impoverished than U.S. natives (Monthly Labor Review, 2003). In fact, between 1994 and 2000, overall poverty levels dropped in country. This is data from the Bureau of Labor Statistics from 2003:

Figure 5: Poverty Rate Percentage

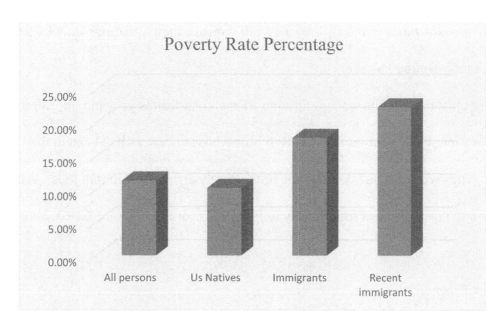

Several times, I recall my parents falling into debt because times were tough, and money was scarce. However, my parents' financial situation improved over time as my dad acquired more language skills and learned to navigate the systems effectively. He acquired enough knowledge to go into another field of work that paid him more money and gave him more financial independence. When we first came to the United States, he was a mechanic. He changed locations and jobs a few times in his career, but he was always a mechanic until my early twenties. When he decided to get licensed to become a truck driver, he started making more money. The additional monthly funds helped him acquire his own truck to become an owner-operator. The networks my father built – people who could help him figure out how he could become a trucker and help him get licensed were a tremendous help to his financial improvement. He took advantage of the opportunities presented to him – he realized the American Dream.

Causes of Poverty

Sometimes when I meet adults who have just immigrated to the United States, I start to think about the difficult times and hardships they are enduring. I try to help them navigate through the various systems in the U.S. so they can improve their situations little by little, especially for their children's sake.

It is not just immigrants who go through financial hardships growing up. While serving in public education, I came across thousands of kids whose ancestors had been in the U.S. for generations. They were just as poor as some of the newly arrived immigrant kids. What causes people to go into poverty varies from family to family. According to compassion.com, poverty is caused by:

- Lack of shelter

- Limited access to clean water

- Food insecurity

- Physical disabilities

- Lack of access to health care

- Unemployment

- Absence of social services

- Gender discrimination

- Poor infrastructure

- Government corruption

- Environmental circumstances

It is important to note that the site also explains other intangible and internal elements cause poverty, including:

- Knowledge

- Aspiration

- Diligence

- Confidence

- Leadership styles

- Social capital

- Values

- Peace

In other words, sometimes people are poor because they simply do not have a choice. They are born into conditions that cause their situations to be so and can do almost nothing to escape them. This situation is common in third-world countries. The conditions are so bad that people risk their lives to travel to other countries where the opportunities to grow and prosper are more accessible.

Other times, people are poor because they can move up and advance with their financial situations but choose not to because of internal factors. They lack motivation, self-confidence, self-discipline, etc. They know they can do better if they apply themselves but choose not to do what it takes due to a lack of diligence and persistence.

Lessons We Learn Climbing Up the Income Ladder

What I learned from living in poverty was not money management or financial planning; I knew to push myself hard to get out of poverty by following the advice of others around me who had been there and done that. In sixth grade, my teacher explained that many students who persevered and earned good grades were often allowed to go to college through scholarships! She told us that college would open doors to financial freedom and independence. She shared how she made a good living and had a home, nice clothing, a car, and vacation money because she had gone to school, earned a degree, and become a teacher. I also witnessed first-hand how the men and women I knew in my circles were successful because they went to college. The education, skills, and certifications they earned helped them to move ahead in life and succeed financially. I decided that I wanted to do the same.

I managed to attend university with a scholarship for four years upon graduating. I was working full-time and going to school full-time, which meant I had a certain amount of control over my personal finances. I was on my own to figure out how I would make my financial ends meet as a young adult. This is when the peak of my own worst financial crisis took plac

The Effects of Debt Accumulation

On many college and university grounds, banking institutions set tables throughout campuses offering young people the opportunities to open credit cards to start building credit. I applied for several of them while I attended Cal. State LA. The credit cards I got made me believe I had money in my pocket. Suddenly, I could buy what I wanted, put it on a charge card, and pay later. I was going to the mall and spending way more than I should have on clothes and shoes. It felt great buying and wearing things that made me feel like I was worth something in my mind.

"You might be poor, your shoes might be broken, but your mind is a palace." -Frank McCourt

I applied for more and more credit cards, including ones from department stores. About a year into spending, I felt a financial crunch. It was apparent that my income was disappearing from me. Where was all that money going? Why did I feel like I was choking and in constant need of money at such a young age?

I will never forget that one Saturday at work, around 1:00 pm. I worked from 9 am to 1 pm on Saturdays. I had every one of my bills with me, and I was determined to sit down and figure out what was happening with my finances. I added up all the money I owed to credit card companies, the monthly interest payments, and how much of my income was going to pay down debt. I was stunned by my findings. I was 21 years old and $22,000 in debt.

Once I saw what was happening with my finances, I was traumatized, worried, and disappointed in myself. I decided to become highly self-disciplined with money and pay off the entire amount in an organized and efficient manner. I devised a game plan and a specific timeline for paying off the debt. Within a few years, the entire amount of credit card debt was paid off, and I was in a position where I could start saving a bit for my future.

"I come from the slums; I come from a hard background; I come from a poor family; and I was a solder." -Michael Caine

Looking back, I am unsure if I had learned more about financial management, proper spending, and adequate saving of money at a young age would have helped me avoid what I went through when I was 21 and in significant credit card debt. I am not sure if my lack of knowledge of personal financial management was an issue or my image of myself as a person who was "worth less" because I did not grow up with money.

Research shows that people in poverty enter a scarcity mindset. They focus on short-term survival, meaning their money decisions are narrowed (Theguardian.com, 2015). Their spending habits indicate that they are trying to satisfy their immediate needs of "today," not "tomorrow," which explains why I spent so much money in short periods to meet some internal needs.

The more damaging aspect of poverty is how people feel about themselves when they are poor (Theguardian.com, 2015). They are less confident in their ability to succeed. Because of that, they have a negative self-image and decreased professional and educational attainment, which may lead to depression and anxiety. They even develop a self-loathing subconsciousness. It was not until I got into heavy debt in my early twenties that my issue was this: I was comparing myself to other kids with more money and self-confidence in high school. This feeling may have led to my uncontrollable spending later as a young adult.

The cycle of poverty is a vicious one. The psychological impact of poverty is so severe, especially for young people, that it's hard to convince themselves that they can break out of that cycle as long as they believe in themselves, apply themselves, and build self-confidence. This goes back to what was said at this chapter's beginning – educating kids at a young age. Whether a child is growing up in a low-income or middle-income home, teaching the value of money is of utmost importance.

As I mentioned earlier in this chapter, teaching kids the basics of money management is important and necessary to help them make good decisions later in life. We have to teach them to learn from our mistakes. It's not just about teaching kids the value of money, spending, and saving. We must give kids the encouragement and motivation to strive and work hard to realize their dreams and achieve their financial goals. Children can learn from positive role models to take on opportunities to acquire more skills and knowledge in life. Those skills and that knowledge can open up doors to better living conditions.

I could not write this book had I not experienced the problems and issues of my past. Having persevered through those hardships has helped me design strategies, ideas, and concepts that I can now share with struggling others. The biggest takeaway from my past, has been the development of proper organizational skills with finances. Those skills have helped me manage money better over the years.

I cannot say that money is no object for me; it most certainly is. I am still on a strict monthly budget to ensure I have enough for emergencies, monthly spending, fun activities, and saving. Having struggled in the past has made me realize that I could fall right back into that cycle if I am not organized and self-disciplined with my money. The lessons from our past always help us make informed decisions for the future!

Strategies, Ideas, and Steps to Improving Personal Finances

Based on what has been shared in this chapter, some strategies and ideas can help keep us all on track with better money management. All actions and steps shown in each chapter can be found in Chapter 9 accumulated altogether.

- ☐ *If I am in debt, I will put together a document together showing how much I owe and how much I am spending paying off debt each month.*

- ☐ *If I have small credit card balances, I will focus on paying them off one by one. I will make smaller payments on the more significant card balances until I pay off the smaller ones.*

- ☐ *To pay off debt, I will look at every item I pay money for each month and adjust. The money I save on other things will go directly into paying the debt. For example, if I reduce my cable bill by $23.00, I will ensure that $23.00 goes directly toward a credit card balance.*

☐ *I will not completely cut off all enjoyments I get out of life to pay off debt because complete depravity is not the way to go. I will, however, curtain some actions and activities. For example, instead of getting a Frappuccino every other day, I will only get one per week, or better yet, one every two weeks.*

☐ *I will try to change my debt balances to a credit card with a much lower interest rate or negotiate with the existing credit card company to reduce the rate as much as possible.*

☐ *When I get a more considerable sum of money at once, like tax returns or birthday gifts, I will pay most of it toward debt.*

☐ *I will give myself a small celebration as I pay off each credit card debt. For example, I can get a small dessert from somewhere to enjoy, get a pedicure, or go to the beach for a day.*

☐ *I will use an Excel sheet to keep all finances organized or paper forms. There are debt trackers and personal financial templates that are helpful and useful if I research to find them. I can even purchase them for $1.00 or $2.00 on efficiencyandorganization.com/products.*

☐ *I will teach my children, grandchildren, nieces, or nephews about money matters. I will ask them what they know about debt, income, expenses, etc. I will help them figure out how they can learn more about personal finances.*

☐ *I will research once a month to learn about debt-reducing strategies.*

☐ *I will have 3 specific goals that I track each month for my personal financial success. Here are examples:*

> *I will save $1,600 to get two doors replaced in my home within one year.*

I will put a limit and spend no more than $600 on clothes and shoes in the next 12 months.

I will take a free or low-fee college class to acquire more skills and knowledge to help me get a promotion and earn more money within the next two years.

Conclusion

Debt is not necessarily a bad thing – many of the most successful companies in the world once started by borrowing money to build their buildings and facilities. Debt is sometimes just part of life for us individuals, too, not just large organizations. As long as we are responsible with borrowing money, we can pay off quickly and efficiently, whether it's student loans, business startup loans, or mortgages. If debt is used to invest for the future, it's okay to acquire it. The key is to make sure to control it and borrow reasonable amounts.

The problem with debt is when it is accumulated by purchasing things that are unnecessary and outside of our buying power. Buying a $ 10,000 diamond ring or a $ 2,000 purse is not wise on a total annual income of $30,000. Getting the object helps us feel good – almost giving us a sense of power. The feeling goes away soon after the credit card bill arrives for the purchase that we could not afford to make in the first place.

Having worked in the public school systems with students in impoverished areas over the past 13 years, I have seen how much kids struggle financially in their households, just like my family and I used to struggle. I feel their pain and see how much they yearn to have more. Teaching and advising kids through examples and first-hand experiences is key to helping them avoid financial troubles in the future. We can become more educated about spending money effectively and efficiently by learning from past mistakes, and the experiences of others around us. We can read self-help books, get sound advice, and set realistic financial goals to achieve.

Chapter 3
Financial Organization and Goals

Becoming organized with finances is one of the first steps to learn about where we were, where we are, and where we want to go with our income, expenses, and investments. There are simple tools and strategies to become more financially organized and efficient.

The Past

We must ask ourselves some critical questions about our past spending and savings habits. Those questions will help determine where we want to be in the present and the future:

- What purchases did we make in the past that we now regret?

- What financial decisions have we made that we are now proud of?

- What are some spending habits and saving habits from the past that we want to continue into the future?

- Do we have debt accumulated from the past that we want to get rid of soon?

Looking at past financial decisions and behaviors to guide where we want to be in the future is essential. This is especially true if we are still dealing with past financial decisions. For example, if we have certain debts and investments, we need to consider how we can deal with them in the present and the future. We can use a simple T-chart to determine the financial behaviors and decisions that we want to keep from the past and the ones we want to change:

Figure 6: Past Financial Decisions and Actions

Past Financial Decisions and Actions	
Positive	**Negative**

Here is an example:

Figure 7: Examples of Past Financial Decisions and Actions

Past Financial Decisions and Actions	
Positive	**Negative**
Paid bills on time – almost always	*Borrowed too much money – credit card debt*
Often bought food from discount grocery stores or with coupons	*Did not do enough research before buying a new car*
Managed to save enough to go on a small trip each year	*Did not budget properly for vacations – overspent during vacations*

There are past financial decisions and actions that we have and should keep or cultivate for the future! We can list as many items as we would like on each side. We must remember not to be too tough on ourselves and list only negative items.

Our past will dictate how much we owe to various institutions – our total debt. We can use an application like Microsoft Excel, or even a Word document to jot down all types of loans and monies we owe. Figuring out where we are with all debt (car loans, home loans, credit card debt, personal loans, student loans) will help us see the big picture moving forward.

Figure 8: Total Debt Finder

Total Debt Finder				
Student Loans	**Personal Loans**	**Car Loans**	**Credit Cards**	**Other Debt**
Amount owed:	Amount owed:	Amount owed:	Amount owed:	Amount owed:
Amount of interest paid each month:	Amount of interest paid each month:	Amount of interest paid each month:	Amount of interest paid each month:	Amount of interest paid each month:

One of the biggest pitfalls of most middle-income American families is controlling personal debt. Being able to analyze total debt visually is necessary. As difficult as it may be, let's sit down and write out what is owed, to whom, and what institution to tackle the problem head-on by coming up with a game plan to pay down debt.

The Present

Once the past is analyzed, we can look at the present and figure out what we want to do immediately to help our situations. We can ask ourselves questions to determine what we want to do to improve our financial position and prepare for the future. Here are some sample questions:

Figure 9: Financial Questionnaire

Financial Questionnaire
1) How much money do I want to have saved in the bank?
2) How much cash do I want to have saved in my home?
3) Do I have some jewelry, guns, bikes, tools, or other items I can sell and get money for?
4) Do I want to make some major repairs or remodeling to my home?
5) Do I want to own more than one property in the future?
6) Do I need to save money for my kids' future?
7) When do I need to purchase another car?
8) Do I need to save money to continue my education or get student loans?
9) By when should I have each of my debts (other than home loan) paid?
10) Do I want to save money to start my own business?
11) Do I want to investigate investing in stocks and bonds? If so, with how much money?
12) What are 5 things I can do to save money each month on food, bills, etc.

13) Do I have the right amount of life insurance in place?
14) Do I have the right amount of home insurance, flood insurance, earthquake insurance?
15) What can I do to increase my monthly income?
16) Have I investigated refinancing any of my debt to reduce interest rates?
17) Do I know exactly how much money I get from each paycheck and how much goes out?
18) Do I have a monthly budget plan to figure out how much is going out how my money is being spent each month?
19) Do I have money in a retirement account? If not, will social security income be enough for me to live on when I can't work anymore?
20) Other?

By answering these questions, we can figure out what financial goals we want to start working on immediately and in the future. Unless we ask ourselves some questions, we cannot determine where we want to be in the near and distant future.

The Future

Our financial future is all about setting financial goals. The process has five essential steps:

1) Visualize success

2) Set specific goals

3) Set specific action plans for each goal

4) Monitor each goal consistently

5) Celebrate the small wins

Figure 10: Goal Achievement Process

Goal Achievement Process

Formulate your vision of success: How does it feel achieving success with what you want to achieve?

Write specific action plans that must be completed with deadlines in order to achieve the overarching goal.

Celebrate your success and move on to a new goal!!!

Write a SMART goal: It needs to be realistic, attainable, measurable, and timely.

Monitor your progress every week, every 2 weeks, or every month.

An efficient and organized process

Visualizing Success

Visualizing success is the first step because we need to envision what it would be like, at the end, to achieve the goal. How would we feel? How would we look? How would we act? We must capture that feeling of success in our imagination because that will keep us going when we want to give up.

Setting Financial Goals

Once we visualize the feeling of success, we can set specific financial goals. To illustrate, here are three examples.

Figure 10: Financial Goals

Financial Goal #1	Financial Goal #2	Financial Goal #3
Save $1,000 in emergency cash at home by the end of 20 months.	Cut back $100 in monthly bills in the next two months.	Change kitchen cabinets and appliances within 12 months.

Each of the three goals has a specific time factor involved. They derive from the

questionnaire in Figure 8. Each one is specific enough to implement. The first goal has a precise

dollar figure to save in an exact amount of time. The second goal is also precise with an amount

and a due date. The third goal does not have a dollar value associated with it. However, it is

distinct in stating what to accomplish and by what deadline.

Set Specific Action Plans

The action steps give more details in a checklist format for each goal. They break down

the goal into specific steps that can easily be checked off when completed. Most people set goals

in life but rarely accomplish them because they do not have specific actions to take daily or

weekly to achieve the final goal. Being specific is critical.

Figure 11: Financial Goals and Action Plans

Financial Goal #1	Financial Goal #2	Financial Goal #3
Save $1,000 in emergency cash money at home by the end of 20 months.	Cut back $100 in monthly bills in the next 2 months.	Change kitchen cabinets and appliances within 12 months.
Action Plans		
Get an envelope to save the money each month.	Write down every single bill that gets paid each month.	Go to 3 different stores to pick out designs for cabinets and get pricing information.
Put away $50 per month or $25 every 2 weeks.	Look at the bills where to lower costs – cable, telephone, electricity, etc.	Go to 3 different appliance stores to see which brands and colors you want to purchase.

Look at where you need to cut savings to be able to save money toward this goal.	Contact companies to learn how to save by lowering usage or changing plan options.	Research the best times of the year to purchase appliances for the lowest prices.
Any unexpected money that comes in, like birthday or tax return, should go into this fund.	Change plans, if necessary. For example, look for another car insurance company if the current one is expensive to pay each month.	Get three quotes from trusted contractors for the installation process.

There can be several other action plans for each of the goals. The more specific the plans are, the easier it will be to achieve the goal. Breaking down into systematic, smaller steps helps take goals from being just goals to being actionable items.

Monitoring Goals

The fourth step after setting action plans is monitoring the goals, which is another very important step. Having written action plans is 25% of the process. Having action plans is another 25%. Monitoring is 50% of the process because it requires consistency. It is best to have the goals written on a form and placed somewhere that can be easily retrieved and monitored. Monitor each financial goal weekly, biweekly, monthly or quarterly basis. Figure 10 takes the goals, and the action plans then adds the monitoring step to each.

Figure 12: Financial Goals, Action Plans, Monitoring Progress

Financial Goal #1	Financial Goal #2	Financial Goal #3
Save $1,000 in emergency cash money at home by the end of 20 months.	Cut back $100 in monthly bills in the next 2 months.	Change kitchen cabinets and appliances within 12 months.
Action Plans		
Get an envelope to save the money each month.	Write down every single bill that gets paid each month.	Go to 3 different stores to pick out designs for cabinets and get pricing information.
Put away $50 per month or $25 every 2 weeks.	Look at the bills where money can actually be saved	Go to 3 different appliance stores to see which brands

	– cable, telephone, electricity, etc.	and colors you want to purchase.
Look at where you need to cut savings to be able to save the money toward this goal.	Contact companies to learn how money can be saved by lowering usage or changing plan options.	Research to find out the best times of the year to purchase appliances for lowest prices.
Any unexpected money that comes in, like birthday or tax return, should go into this fund.	Change plans, if necessary. For example, look for another car insurance company if the current one is expensive to pay each month.	Get 3 quotes from trusted contractors for the installation process.
Monitoring Frequency		
Monthly	Monthly	Quarterly

Monitoring frequency explains how often the action plans will be revisited to mark as completed. For example, if we are following the action plan by saving toward the $1,000 emergency fund, then progress is being made. No other action plans are needed. If we are falling behind and not saving as much as we set out to do, we must adjust the time or add more action plans to help us save.

For monitoring reasons, we need to have the goals posted somewhere that we can easily see or retrieve. They can be saved on a USB drive or a computer. They can also be printed and posted somewhere easy to find. On the telephone, we can set a reminder each month to remind us to stop and track our progress. Another way to remember to monitor is to use a calendar and planner. Calendaring every week, month, or quarter will help us not forget to stop and look at the action plans for each goal to cross off as we accomplish each.

Celebrating Small Wins

We should reward ourselves whenever we are on track to meet a goal. The celebrations can be small and inexpensive, like eating a favorite snack, going to a coffee shop, or even a pat on the back. The celebrations are ways to reward ourselves for staying on track to meet our goals.

Organizational Tips for Personal Finances

Setting goals requires us to be financially organized, neat, tidy, and decluttered. There are several benefits to being financially organized:

- Easy access to information

- Saving time and energy

- Becoming more efficient

- Having peace of mind

- Increased productivity

- More sense of control (Moneycrashers.com, 2021)

- Less stress and worry

- Less clutter and confusion

- Better money management (Moneywisepastor.com, 2021)

- Stronger sense of accomplishment and self-pride

Figure 13: Benefits of Financial Organization

Here are some strategies, tips, and hacks to stay organized and efficient with accomplishing action plans by monitoring their progress.

- **Keeping financial documents filed temporarily is necessary because we do not know when we will need them.** Prevent clutter by storing documents in either binders or files in a filing cabinet. They can be thrown away after one year, in most cases. The idea is to sort them into categories or by name for easy access. Most people keep their documents, but they are all thrown together in a drawer or cabinet. Then, they go to look for something they need. They get frustrated when they can't find the paperwork quickly enough. We need to fight the urge to procrastinate and organize from the beginning. Doing so will help us to efficiently and speedily retrieve paperwork that we may need in the future.

- **To prevent clutter, we must throw out old forms and documents, such as old utility bills, cable bills, invoices, etc.** Toss away documents to eliminate clutter and confusion.

Some documents, like tax returns, are crucial to keeping for 4 to 7 years. If we are unsure how long to keep those documents, do an online search or ask a professional.

- **Spending time organizing documents can be done daily, weekly, or monthly.** If we take time to sort and categorize, we can make the paperwork manageable, lowering our level of stress and anxiety when it comes to piles of papers all clumped together. There can be an "inbox" to take in all paperwork related to money and bills that arrive each week. Sort away either weekly or monthly, if daily is too time-consuming. Declutter the paperwork and documents.

- **A good way to store information and documents is to scan and save them in folders on USB drives or personal computers.** It takes far less space to store on the computer than in physical files in cabinets. Retrieve documents fast and efficiently with a "Find" search. This might be a viable option, especially for people afraid to throw away anything related to personal finances. Some of the categories can include:
  - Credit card statements
  - Mortgage statements
  - Car registration renewals
  - Gas bills
  - Electric bills
  - Tax returns

Once we upload the documents, we can shred them.

- **Organizing personal finances is doing our bookkeeping.** What bookkeepers do for business owners is, basically, financial organization! They sort receipts, and expenses, track where income comes from, and what sources, etc. Without proper bookkeeping, a business suffers financially. The business owners have no idea what product or service is selling well, which clients have not paid, which bills are not paid, whether taxes are filed properly, etc. Sometimes, businesses have excellent services and products, but due to poor money management, they go bankrupt and out of business! Proper personal bookkeeping works the same way. The more organized we become with our money, the better we can manage it. If the idea of organizing and categorizing is too cumbersome or stressful, we can hire a personal bookkeeper, but we need to understand that the service costs money. If it is worth saving the time and hassle of hiring someone to do the personal financial organizing for us, then hiring a bookkeeper is a good decision.

Strategies, Ideas, and Steps to Improving Personal Finances

Some strategies and ideas listed in this chapter can help keep us all on track with better money management. All actions and steps shown in each chapter can be found in Chapter 9 accumulated altogether.

- *Use a T-chart to determine past financial decisions and actions that are positive and negative.*

- *Use a debt tracker to determine how much is owed for various debts and loans and what the monthly interest amounts paid are.*

- *Give yourself a financial questionnaire to determine what you want to work on immediately to improve your financial situation.*

- *Set 3 to 5 financial goals based on examples in Figure 8 that involve a time factor and are specific in nature.*

- *Set specific action plans for each of the goals.*

- ☐ *Set monitoring frequency to know when to revisit the goal and check off the associated action plans.*

- ☐ *Choose a few organizational tips to implement to stay decluttered, neat, coordinated, and structured with personal finances.*

- ☐ *Organize personal finances by filing money-related documents sorted and filed or saved in files on the computer.*

- ☐ *Declutter and throw out old money-related paperwork once a week, month, or year, or scan and save in folders on the computer or USB drive.*

- ☐ *If doing the financial organization is too stressful a task, hire a bookkeeper to do this for you each month.*

Conclusion

Financial goals and plans help us develop a road map; they help us see where we were, where we are, and where we are going in our financial journey. They also help us break down what we want to achieve in life, financially, into workable chunks. We break down primary goals into smaller, practical, doable pieces that can be implemented individually. It almost becomes like solving a big algebra problem. When we first see the problem, we panic and think it is too complex to solve. As soon as we start working on it step-by-step, we manage to break the problem apart and reach a solution in an organized and systematic fashion!

"Financial success, as well as most success in life, is not about perfection, it's about direction."
-Donald Lynn Frost

When setting financial goals, it is essential to remember that too many will become challenging to implement. Have 3 to 5 goals and set new goals as each one gets accomplished. There are various action steps involved with each goal that will require time to achieve in a timely manner. Set just a few financial goals in addition to the other goals in life, like personal, professional, spiritual, health, and educational goals.

Besides setting financial goals, we also discussed being financially organized in this chapter. There are many benefits to being financially organized. We can prioritize better, have less clutter, more peace of mind, have stronger time management skills, and feel better about ourselves.

Financial organization and goals go together because one gives way for the other. Our goals guide us from where we are to where we want to be! If there is disorder, clutter, and lack of structure, goals cannot be easily set and accomplished.

Chapter 4
Having a Budget

Creating and maintaining a budget is one of the most important things anyone can do to stay organized and well-managed with personal finances. A budget is not just a way to track what is coming and going on each month. It helps plan what income is expected to come in and what expenses are expected to go out. Creating a budget is relatively easy; maintaining a budget is difficult because it involves self-discipline, self-control, and consistency.

According to 60minutefinance.com, some of the top reasons why people refuse to budget include the following:

- They are afraid to face the truth about their finances.

- They don't like to have limits and constraints put on themselves.

- Having a budget has not worked for them in the past.

- They are too proud and convince themselves they do not need to budget because they know how to budget money.

- They are too lazy.

- Since they always have money left in their accounts at the end of the month, they figure they are doing well enough to not need a budget or financial plan each month.

- They are afraid it might lead to marital fights.

- They do not know how to prepare one.

At least one of the reasons listed would resonate with any of us at one point or another. Budgeting takes time and effort but is necessary for our financial health and well-being. Our economic well-being affects our mental well-being!

There are more advantages than disadvantages to budgeting. According to Investopedia.com, budgeting helps with:

- Accomplishing long-term and short-term financial goals

- Ensuring that money is not overspent each month leading a person into debt

- Leading to a happier retirement

- Preparing for emergencies

- Shedding light on bad spending habits

- Getting a better night's sleep due to more inner peace and reassurance

Other experts add their own list of advantages when it comes to budgeting, like Inspiredbudget.com and bethebudget.com:

- Having more emotional security and less stress

- Having more control over money

- Being able to teach our kids about finances

- Getting rid of debt more quickly

- Setting priorities

- Leading to more communication within the family and a happier marriage

- Staying organized

- Saving money

Figure 14: Advantages of Starting and Maintaining a Personal Budget

Advantages of Starting & Maintaining a Personal Budget

Accomplishing long-term and short-term financial goals

Preparing for emergencies

Ensuring that money is not overspent each month leading a person into debt

Leading to a happier retirement

Shedding light on bad spending habits

Getting a better night's sleep due to more inner-peace and reassurance

Having more emotional security and less stress

Having more control over money

Being able to teach your own kids about finances

Getting rid of debt more quickly

Setting priorities

Leading to more communication within the family and a happier marriage

Staying organized

Saving money

The advantages of having a budget far outweigh the disadvantages. Creating a budget is easy. Maintaining one is tricky. Once created, the key is to develop enough self-discipline, self-control, and consistency to stay with it.

Creating a Budget

When creating a budget, we look at the big financial picture – how much money is coming in and how much money is going out. Typically, a simple budget has two columns. A form can be created by hand or using a software program like Excel or Word. Some people like using Quickbooks, but if it takes time to learn a new program, we might as well just stick to the most straightforward way of budgeting by just using what we know already – Microsoft Office

products or a simple pencil and paper.

An Excel document is probably the best way to budget. It has an adding/subtracting

formula. To get a form already set up with formulas and is very basic, please go to

efficiencyandorganization.com/personal-finances. We can also search on the internet or

Pinterest.com for some very easy-to-use budget forms.

Figure 15: Monthly Personal Budget Template

Monthly Personal Budget			
Income		**Expense**	
Source:	$	Type:	$
Source:	$	Type:	$
Source:	$	Type:	$
Source:	$	Type:	$
Source:	$	Type:	$
Source:	$	Type:	$
Source:	$	Type:	$
		Type:	$
		Type:	$
		Type:	$
		Type:	$
		Type:	$
		Type:	$

Total Income: [   ]   Total Expense: [   ]

Income Part of a Budget

The income column may have more than one source if there are various revenue streams.

For example, some families get money from their places of work, social security benefits, and side jobs each month. Others get the same amount each month, except here and there, some additional funds come in, like birthday money, tax refund money, etc. It's essential to include all monies in the income column to know what is coming in and going out down to the last penny. Besides work income, other sources of income include:

- Tax return money

- Gifts

- Rebates

- Dividends or interest money directly placed into our account

- Insurance claim funds

- Money from sales of personal items

- Money from a side business

- Cash refunds

- Money someone owes us and pays us back

- Lottery winnings

- Reimbursements

It is easier to use Excel because the formula for summation can be applied. If not familiar with Excel, a simple Word document can be used or even just paper and pencil! Tabulate the final amounts in the income and expense columns.

Here is an example:

Figure 16: Income Column Template

Income	
Source: work	$5274.72
Source: gift	$50.00
Source: reimbursements from work	$72.13

TOTAL:	$5,396.85

Look at the monthly income for tracking purposes once each month. Monitor the budget each week. Track additional income and expenses to keep records updated. Here are two things to keep in mind:

- **We create a budget once a month, at the beginning of each month.**

- **We track income and expenses at least once each week.**

On the first of each month, we can look at the month ahead and figure out what money we expect will come in the form of income and what money will go out in expenses. The monthly budget allows us to see the big picture for the entire month. It allows us to see what we have coming in and how much we can allow ourselves to spend on expenses and put away in savings, so we do not fall into debt. The two columns must match; in other words, the income must match the payments.

Expenses and Savings Part of a Budget

Expenses can go into another column and can be tracked on a weekly basis. Some expenses stay consistent each month. Examples include the gas bill, the telephone bill, the electric bill. The amounts vary depending on the season, or if there are economic factors, like inflation, that make the amounts due increase. The gas bill, for instance, is less during the summer than during the winter months.

Other expenses may arise that are unexpected or extra. These include:

- Emergency home repairs

- Auto repairs

- Unplanned travel expenses

- Income tax payments

- Medical costs

- Pet emergencies

- Unexpected gifts

- Money lent to close family members due to emergencies

As mentioned previously, there are two essential things to keep in mind with tracking income and expenses:

- **We create a budget once a month, at the beginning of each month.**

- **We track income and expense each week.**

When it comes to expenses, we write down either the exact amounts we need to pay on the first of the month for each item or an estimated payment (if we do not know exactly what the total might be). We track income and expenses each week to slowly turn the *estimated* amounts into *actual* amounts without going over.

Unexpected Expenses

The best way to combat unexpected and sudden expenses is by saving money for emergencies. The amount that gets saved depends on each person's ability. There is no hard-and-fast rule for how much a person should save but basing on a percentage is not a bad idea! Some experts suggest saving 10% of income, while others recommend saving 30%. The amount we save depends on our circumstances and our financial goals. For example, in an article by Moneycrashers.com, when it comes to home repairs, the golden rule is 1% of the sales price of the home for repairs. In other words, if the house is worth $500,000, approximately $5,000 must be set aside for emergencies. Consider saving 2% of the home sales price so the additional funds can cover other emergency expenses.

Another suggestion for dealing with other expenses is building and maintaining good credit. For example, to finance the purchase of a computer, a person with a good credit score should be able to get a rate of 0% for a few months to a few years, allowing more time to make payments. Unfortunately, people with poor credit scores cannot obtain this deal. For them to finance a computer will be more costly, if not impossible.

The expense column can look something like what is shown in Figure 17. The income goes in the left column while the expenses go in the right column. The idea is to match the left bottom line (total) with the right bottom line each month.

Figure 17: Example of a Monthly Personal Budget

Monthly Personal Budget			
Income		**Expense**	
Source: work	$5274.72	Type: electric bill	$112.74
Source: gift	$50.00	Type: cellular	$121.98
Source: reimbursement	$72.13	Type: rent/mortgage	$1850.00
Source:	$	Type: food	$1100.00
Source:	$	Type: car payment	$350.09
Source:	$	Type: credit card	$250.00
Source:	$	Type: household	$200.00
		Type: gas bill	$24.37
		Type: internet	$79.99
		Type: gardener	$75.00
		Type: cable/television	$110.46
		Type: insurance	$122.22
		Type: savings	$500.00
		Type: repairs	$200.00
		Type: health-related	$100.00
		Type: leisure & fun	$200.00

Total Income: $5,396.85 Total Expense: $5396.85

Obligatory expenses must be dealt with before leisure and fun expenses. Obligatory expenses include rent, credit card payments, and utility bills. Leisure expenses include holiday travels, trips to the coffee shop, and cable or streaming services. The only way to increase money for leisurely and fun activities is to save in other areas. The same goes for the savings category. We need to cut costs and expenses to save more money for things we need and want.

If we do not want to cut costs and expenses, we need to generate more money. Income must be increased if costs cannot be cut in other areas. This is the main reason why people often do not budget. They see the harsh reality of their financial situations – they see the big picture, which makes them upset. They feel restricted and constricted by their situation.

Let's face it; budget *IS* a way for us to restrict and confine ourselves to spending and saving based on our current financial abilities. Therefore, it takes self-discipline and self-control. Fortunately, we can help each other and learn from one another when building more self-discipline and self-control! If we are all doing this together and helping one another through the journey of reaching financial success, then we CAN increase our incomes if we want; we CAN increase our savings and reduce our expenses!

Savings Part of a Budget

Emergencies and other unexpected expenses are not the only reasons why people save. Some other reasons include:

- Vacations
- Retirement
- Large purchases, like furniture, cars, boats, homes
- Gift money to others

- School/college

- Home repairs and remodeling

- Cosmetic surgeries

Some people include the amount they save each month in the expense column. The reason is that they see it as money that is being taken out of their income that cannot be touched. That's actually a pretty smart move! Another approach is to have a separate column for savings, or savings can be taken out from the beginning and not be entered into the budget form.

People save money in a variety of ways. Here are some examples:

- Calculating the percentage of income to put in savings

- Setting aside a fixed amount once a month

- Putting away a fixed amount every paycheck

- Putting away only monies that are unexpected or extra each month

- Having the banking institution take money automatically from the checking account each month

- Having some cash saved at home and the rest in an account at the bank

There are various ways to save money. Whichever method we choose is up to us, as long as we save, not just for emergencies, but for other aspects of life, too! These include:

- Savings account at the bank (or separate accounts – one for each saving goal)

- Cash in an envelope at home (or a few envelopes – one for each saving goal)

- Giving money to a trusted family member to save for us

Self-Discipline and Self-Control

It is challenging to have self-discipline and self-control with money. When we see others around us buying brand-new cars, new clothes, new shoes, and more, we often want the same.

We buy things on credit and take out loans when we cannot afford the same luxuries as others. We often feel bad for ourselves, and our self-esteem drops when we cannot afford things we want. Life really is not fair sometimes. Some people can afford some things that others of us cannot. However, telling ourselves that is not going to change anything. It is just going to get us to make excuses for ourselves to continue the victim mentality. According to healthline.com, victim mentality is when we think:

- Bad things keep happening and will continue to happen

- Other people or and outside circumstances are to blame for our misfortunes

- There is no point in trying because no matter what we do, we are going to fail

Thinking negatively will only make matters worse and not allow us to try. We must change our thoughts. If we want more, we must earn more. The first step in generating more money each month and being self-disciplined with how we spend and save. We need to stop comparing ourselves to others because, in reality, "the grass is not greener on the other side." Some people are indeed born with more resources and abilities, but most people achieve financial success by focusing on saving, earning more, and controlling spending; in other words, having self-discipline and self-control.

"Discipline is money in the bank." – Henry Rollins

Despite what others say, do, or have, we must tell ourselves that we can do it – we can save, and we can learn more skills to get better jobs. We can have self-control and self-discipline. We can start side businesses and put effort into growing them to generate profit. We can save more – even if it is just a little bit of money each month. We can use these self-affirming statements once weekly to convince ourselves that we can and will!

Figure 18: Self-Affirmation Statements to Earn More, Save More, and Spend Less

Self-affirmation Statements to Earn More, Save More, and Spend Less

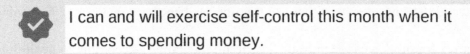
✔ I can and will exercise self-control this month when it comes to spending money.

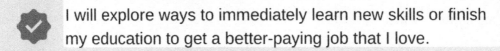
✔ I will explore ways to immediately learn new skills or finish my education to get a better-paying job that I love.

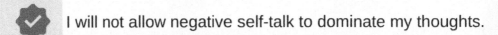
✔ I will not allow negative self-talk to dominate my thoughts.

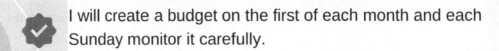
✔ I will create a budget on the first of each month and each Sunday monitor it carefully.

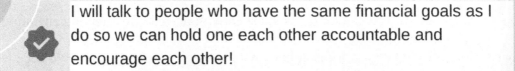
✔ I will talk to people who have the same financial goals as I do so we can hold one each other accountable and encourage each other!

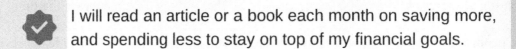
✔ I will read an article or a book each month on saving more, and spending less to stay on top of my financial goals.

✔ I will create 3 to 5 short-term and long-term financial goals and hold myself accountable for achieving them.

efficiencyandorganization.com

The biggest disappointment for most people is seeing how little money they have to spend on leisure and fun. This is the discretionary part of the budget. They work so hard all week and want to generate enough income to splurge when they want to on fun things.

Life is stressful for most people because there is too much to balance – work, family, school, side business, home, finances, repairs, plans for the future, health, and so much more. Life is incredibly stressful when outside forces affect our mental and physical health, like illnesses, economic downturns, severe weather, etc. We deal with stress by self-soothing, sometimes by spending money on leisurely things, like going out to fancy restaurants, buying an expensive piece of jewelry, an expensive purse, or the latest and greatest cellular phone.

Having middle-class income means having to budget, having short-term and long-term financial goals, and consistently following through with them in an organized and efficient manner. If we set financial goals and stick to them, we can generate more income, spend less, and save more. We can even increase our spending on leisure and fun if we are disciplined enough to save.

Consistency

It is easier to set goals, create budgets, and establish plans than to follow through with them. We can tell ourselves that we will create an organized system for budgeting each month, but are we going to follow through with the budget plan or will we ignore it once it is written? This is where consistency plays a role. There cannot just be a plan; there needs to be an organized and efficient way to consistently follow through with the plan.

"Small disciplines repeated with consistency every day lead to great achievements gained slowly over time." – John C. Maxwell

One of the most important ways to be consistent with money management is to use a planner and a calendar. A planner and a calendar help maintain consistency with financial goals and budgets. These two tools combined are beneficial in many aspects of life for organizing.

On the first day of each month, create or edit the budget for the entire month. Have the income and expenses listed to develop a spending and saving plan. Each Sunday, take 30 minutes to review and make changes as necessary. For example, if the budget for the telephone bill was $121.98, but it was $118.15, adjust. If the total food costs for the week past were

$213.42, adjust. Use receipts from stores and the checking account statement online from the bank to make the adjustments and ensure the spending plan is on budget.

Another way to be consistent is to stick to our budget. If we agree to spend only $1,200 on food this month, we must stay within that amount. If we decide to put $50 per month in savings for the next 12 months, we must stick to that. Over time, consistency in sticking with these budgeting goals will pay off.

Strategies, Ideas, and Steps to Improving Personal Finances

Based on what has been shared in this chapter, some strategies and ideas can help keep us all on track with better money management. All actions and steps shown in each chapter can be found in Chapter 9 accumulated altogether.

- ☐ *Make a two-column budget for yourself or download one that you can use every week to calculate income and expenses.*

- ☐ *On the first of each month, write in your planner or calendar that you must create the budget with expected income and expenses for that month.*

- ☐ *For the income column, on the first of the month, write down the exact amounts you expect to get in the form of income that month and estimated amounts (if any).*

- ☐ *For the expense column, on the first of the month, write down the exact amounts and estimated amounts for each type of expense you will have that month.*

- ☐ *Make sure you account for how much you expect or plan on saving that month when you set up your budget for the first month.*

- ☐ *Look at every one of the expenses and see how you can cut costs, if at all. Then, make calls or go online to figure out what you need to do to make those savings immediately.*

☐ *Select a specific day of the week to review the budget – income versus expenses. Selecting a particular day and even an exact time of day will increase organization and consistency.*

Conclusion

Creating a budget can be simple enough with a T-chart that includes two columns, one for income and one for expenses. Stick with a monthly budget and monitor carefully. Keep working on developing a stronger self-discipline and self-control. Through consistency, follow a budget and implement it correctly.

The need to set aside money for emergencies and unexpected expenses cannot be understated. Often, these emergency expenses are what throw people into poverty unexpectedly. Having proper insurance, a decent savings plan, and a plan for the unexpected will help us who dwell with middle-income lifestyles maintain them and increase our wealth over time. Dealing with financial emergencies is discussed in upcoming chapters.

Chapter 5
Building and Maintaining Income

When we start to budget, we often realize that to maintain the same lifestyle and not go into debt, we probably need to generate more income. It is a harsh reality when it becomes apparent that we are overspending and need to cut down on some expenses. Either we must go cut back on certain purchases to save money, or we need to generate more income. Cutting back can be daunting, making us upset, sad, and even depressed. We work hard all week long, and when we see that we need to cut back on things we enjoy, it can be painful! Cutting back usually, means cutting non-discretionary items, like:

- Cable or television programs

- How often we go to the movies

- How often we go out to eat

- How often we go on weekend getaways

- Types of meats we purchase to barbeque

- Number of shoes we can purchase

- How much we can donate or give in terms of gifts

- Membership fees

If we want to maintain the same lifestyle and not make any cutbacks, we need to think about generating more money. Generating more money could come in various forms:

- Salary increases

- Promotions

- Job changes

- Getting a second job

- Starting side businesses

- Becoming self-employed

- Investing in high-risk but short-term investments

We will take a deeper look at each category to generate more money. There may be more ways to increase income that are not listed or discussed here, which we can explore as possible revenue sources.

Salary Increases

Some people have their salaries increase automatically on a set schedule by their employers. Firefighters, police officers, accounting firms, and many other institutions automatically give annual raises with a positive evaluation. Also, there are usually increases to employee payroll when the economy changes, and inflation rises. This is referred to as COLA, or cost of living allowance.

Not all companies offer COLA, and some people do the same job for the same pay year after year without seeing any increases. When we are stuck in these types of jobs, we have a choice to make. We can either ask for a raise or look to find work elsewhere. Whether we get the raise or not depends on the employer. If we are not going to look elsewhere, we have to figure out other ways to generate additional income to sustain our lifestyle and spending. We might have to look to get a second job or start a business that would eventually earn more money.

It is uncomfortable for most people to approach supervisors to ask for raises. We often feel that we deserve it and should not have to ask for a raise. However, most employers usually look at their bottom line when it comes to their finances. Even a $0.25 hourly increase could cost them more than $600 annually. Giving a raise like this to many others within the organization could cost thousands of dollars. They need to be careful with their income and finances, so sometimes their hands are tied. Other times, employers can pay for raises but choose to be selfish. They would rather spend money on unnecessary purchases or give themselves lavish bonuses while keeping employee salaries low. As employees, we must understand that we are not mandated to work at those organizations and have a choice. We must look out for our well-being and what suits our needs. If we need to generate more money, we must figure out what move to make if a salary increase is impossible.

Promotions

A promotion is a practical way to increase salaries or hourly wages. It is an option for a person looking to get more pay! The problem with a promotion is it often comes with additional responsibilities. Many promotional opportunities are in leadership positions. Anyone who has served in a leadership capacity would describe the experience as stressful, at times, and filled with high expectations from upper management. We need to decide whether we are ready and willing to face the challenges of more responsibilities. It may not be the best decision to take on a more significant challenge because it pays us more money.

Promotions typically involve doing the same work but in an advanced role. Here are some examples:

- Accounts receivable clerk to an accountant

- Cashier to lead cashier

- Backup performer to lead performer

- Clerk to secretary

- Warehouse worker to shift leader

- Teacher aide to teacher

- Retail clerk to department supervisor

If a promotion is something worth trying to you as an individual, here is a step-by-step process we need to take to pursue it:

1) Look at the job description to check the minimum requirements.

2) Include minimum requirements in the resume verbatim.

3) If minimum requirements are not met (licensing, certificates, etc.), immediately look for step-by-step strategies for earning them – college, vocational school, training program, etc.

4) Include in the resume some of the typical job duties in the experience section.

5) Write a letter of introduction, even if it is not required for the job.

6) Decide how the promotion will help the organization. Mention that either in the Objective section of the resume or in the introduction letter. Remember, the organization we work for is not there to fulfill our own personal needs. It exists to meet and grow its needs. We must clarify how and why we would be a great asset to the organization by going to the next level in our careers. What are we bringing to the table after a promotion?

7) Talk to network within the organization, especially management, to express interest in a promotion. Specifically ask for expectations and needs that need to be met to go to the next level.

8) Ask about additional duties and assignments to learn that will lead to the next step in the organization; in other words, learn the next set of skills needed to earn a promotion

Some people get promoted within organizations after some years of training and experience. They get promotions if they have a good reputation and are trusted by managers and supervisors. Therefore, having a good reputation within an organization is so incredibly important. However, some promotions cannot be achieved simply by experience and reputation. Some specialized training or licensing is required. For example, a teacher's aide cannot simply become a teacher (next level up). Credentials are required. A certified nursing assistant cannot just become a nurse. Training and licensing are required. If we have any desire to move up and be promoted soon, we need to look at the requirements to meet them when the opportunity presents itself.

Job Changes

There are several other reasons why people change jobs other than for monetary gain:

- Their organizations are toxic

- They may have poor reputations that are preventing them from being chosen for promotions

- Their organization is too small and there are no opportunities for growth

- Their work is not valued or appreciated

- The work is not rewarding or giving them value

When people are looking at making a career or job change, it must benefit them financially, emotionally, and physically. The tricky part about the change is the fear of the unknown. We do not know if the new organization would be a good fit. We do not know if we will like the job or the environment. We may even experience fear of not meeting the expectations of the new position. There is worry and stress involved with a job change. However, if the benefits outweigh the costs, it is worth it! Here are some questions to ask when making a job change offer. If there are no "yes" responses versus "no" responses, it's time to

step out of the comfort zone and go for it.

Figure 19: Job Change Self-Questionnaire

Question	Yes	No
I will earn more money.		
I can develop professionally.		
I will leave an unhealthy or toxic environment at my current job.		
I will have more opportunities.		
I will have more flexibility.		
I will have better benefits.		
Leadership at a new organization will suit my personality more.		
I am dissatisfied with the lack of rewards at my current job.		
I want a fresh new start in my career.		
I want to make a difference and contribute more at my new job.		
Totals (how many "yes" responses vs. how many "no" responses)		

The hardest part about making a job change is it is time-consuming and difficult,

especially if there is a lack of experience. Organizations often do not want to take a chance and

hire someone who may have the licensing and education but not enough experience. There are

some things that formal education cannot or will not teach; knowledge comes from experience.

It might take time to find an organization that will take a chance, or it may require a person to

drive further for a new job or even move to a new state. This sometimes happens with teachers

who want to become principals. It is hard for district officials to give them the opportunity because the teacher may have the credential and degree for the new position but, with a lack of experience, cannot handle the high-stakes job. Thus, teachers apply within a larger radius, knowing there may be a long commute or even moving required. It may also take time. Some teachers apply over and over again. Their job search takes two to three years, if not more, until a job change finally comes their way.

Most promotions we seek move us into leadership positions. We may have the knowledge and skill to do a great job at our current position, but not necessarily in a leadership position. To move up, we must develop better people skills and leadership skills.

Getting a Second Job

If it is going to be difficult and time-consuming to get a promotion or change jobs, there may be a need to get a second job. A large percentage of individuals have either second jobs or side businesses to generate extra income. Some even do seasonal work. They have a full-time job but choose to do taxes during tax season in the early part of the year, or work in retail stores the end of the year. The extra money helps pay for costs and generate some money for disposable income.

The biggest challenge with getting a second job is time management. Most people work these jobs on weekends, evenings, or during hours that do not conflict with their regular place of employment. If a person already has a full-time job or attends school while working, adding another job to the schedule will be challenging and stressful. However, getting a second job may be worthwhile if the long-term benefits outweigh the costs.

If we need to generate some extra funds to get our finances in order and pay off debt, it may be worthwhile looking into getting a second job temporarily. This can be a short-term solution until we acquire the skills and experience necessary to earn a promotion at work or until we find another job that pays better and has other benefits we seek.

Starting a Side Business

Rather than working a second job, some people choose to start a side business or side hustle. For example, a secretary might start a hair styling business. A real estate agent might drive for Uber or Lyft as a side business. Here are some things to know about side businesses:

- They almost always require some type of monetary investment. Even getting a license to operate the business will cost money.

- Licensing or permits may be required. The process could take time and money.

- There may be a need to get credit card processing services, business checking accounts, high-speed internet, a computer with a printer, supplies, and more.

- No money may be generated for a while until clientele is established. For example, if a food server wants to start a side business as a tax preparer, it might take time to advertise, do outreach, and get clientele. In the long run, advertising and marketing might cost money initially, but pay off.

- Because it is a side business, the owner may be overstretched with time and energy and not give the business the time and attention it needs to grow over time. Starting a business is like having a baby; growing requires time, money, energy, love, and patience.

It is imperative to research and write a realistic business plan before starting a side business. We might want to start something not in demand in our area. For example, becoming a massage therapist to earn extra money might sound good, but it might not work out if we cannot get clients who demand the service. Researching will also indicate the licensing and fees required to establish the business. For instance, most cities do not allow homes to be used for business purposes where clients come in and out all day. Houses cannot be set up as shops, either. If a person is a clothing designer and wants to make and sell shirts out of the home, this may not be allowed by the city where she lives.

Most entrepreneurs start side businesses that develop and thrive in about five years. They quit their day jobs and pursue the business on a full-time basis. This is a smart approach because the first few years of a business are complex. There needs to be investment going into the side business until it is established enough to survive on its own financially and generate income for the owner.

To generate extra money to improve our financial standing, we need to carefully consider the advantages and disadvantages of a side business operation. We need to be very careful with time management, planning, and organization to make having a side business work to generate additional income.

Becoming Self-Employed

Some people get so fed up with their jobs that they quit and become self-employed. A person may choose to quiet and start a business if there is strong demand for the product and service he is selling. If he can generate enough income to survive and thrive within the first year of become self-employed, yes! Pursuing one's own business is the way to go!

Most startups will take time to grow to generate enough to live on. Self-employed individuals usually keep their jobs while they do their side business on a part-time basis to develop enough financial resources to survive the first few years while the business grows. A business does not need to begin from scratch; there are startups and established companies that a person can purchase. Startups are challenging because it takes years to see enough income to sustain a comfortable lifestyle. An established business could help generate income immediately but might mean a significant investment upfront. The business's seller will most likely ask for a significant financial investment upfront. If the financial resources are not enough, this might be a problem.

Some established businesses are franchises. For example, Subway, Chick Fill-A, and Domino's are franchises. Franchisedirect.com lists McDonald's as the world's biggest franchiser, followed by KFC, Burger King, and 7-Eleven. Purchasing a franchise has licensing requirements, financial investment, and rules and procedures. Because franchises have more of an established name, getting clients in the door is easier. The first few years of operating might still be financially challenging until the business is more established in the area.

As a person with a middle-class income, choosing to become self-employed is a good idea for the long run, but not necessarily to generate vast amounts of income in the short run.

Investing in High-Risk but Short-Term Investments

The problem with most short-term, high-yield investments is they are often high-risk. Most people do this in terms of buying stocks, for example. They buy stocks in a company that they think will double in value in less than a year. If they do double, then they are in luck! If not, they could end up losing money instead of winning it. Some people gamble large sums of money, hoping they get lucky and their investment doubles, triples, or increases exponentially. Again, this is a high-risk situation. The investment can be gone before we know it.

People with middle-class income cannot afford to lose money. The best option is to think long-term and plan. Whether starting a business, getting a promotion, or changing jobs, success is far more likely if planned ahead.

Coming Across Unexpected Money

Since we are on the topic of income, let us not forget about unexpected money that might come our way at some point in our lives. An old relative can pass away, leaving us with property or cash. We could get a larger-than-expected tax refund. We can get settlement money from a class-action lawsuit. There is an episode of *Seinfeld* in which George Costanza comes across a sum of about $1,900. The interest alone turned that small amount into almost $2,000. Talk about unexpected money! Unexpected money can also be in the form of gifts. My grandmother, for example, gave each of her grandchildren $1,000 when we were teenagers. That was undoubtedly sudden and unexpected money.

"Do not save what is left after spending, but spend what is left after saving." – Warren Buffet

When we get unexpected funds, it is important to put the majority of it toward something meaningful and worthwhile. Yes, it is also necessary to splurge a little by going on a small get-away, going to a fancy dinner, buying a piece of jewelry we have been wanting, and so forth. The majority of the funds, though, should either be saved, used to pay off debt, or used for something important, like home repairs, car repairs, etc. Planning requires self-discipline and self-control. These two key attributes can help take us from where we are now financially to where we need to be – how we invest money. Self-discipline and self-control with money cannot be understated. When people dwell in poverty, money is exceedingly difficult to come by, and when a sudden and unexpected amount comes their way, they often spend it on things they should not. Getting ahead financially is quite challenging. They cannot get themselves out of their financial rut because they do not invest in themselves to generate more income. They do not save for "rainy days." They do not care for the most important things, like repairing their cars to go back and forth to work or school. They do not purchase insurance for their belongings in cases of emergency.

Since this book is being written specifically for people with a middle-class income, it is important to note that not taking care of essential things could push us into poverty. We may lose our homes if we do not have proper home or earthquake insurance coverage and a disaster occurs. If we do not take care of our health insurance needs and end up in a hospital, we might be pushed into poverty and bankruptcy over the high healthcare costs. If our car breaks down and we cannot afford to rent a car temporarily, borrow a car, or get our car repaired/replaced, we cannot go to work and face losing our jobs. Since we are in the middle class, let us not forget we are just a few steps away from going into poverty if we do not take care of our finances. However, we are also a few steps away from achieving even more income and wealth – going into the upper middle class or the wealthy category. Managing personal finances is crucial to our overall mental and physical health and well-being. This starts with handling unexpected income wisely and efficiently.

Strategies, Ideas, and Steps to Improving Personal Finances

Here are some strategies and ideas that can help keep us all on track with better money management discussed in this chapter. All actions and steps shown in each chapter can be found in Chapter 9 accumulated altogether.

- ☐ *If I receive unexpected funds, I will either save, pay off debt, or use it for something important, like home repairs, car repairs, going into a certification program, etc.*

- ☐ *I will read a book this year that can help me shift from having a negative mindset to having more confidence in myself to earn more money and increase my income.*

- ☐ *I will review my insurance policies within two months to ensure I am adequately covered. I will contact my insurance broker for advice.*

- ☐ *In the next three months, I will carefully consider ways to generate or earn more income to realize my full financial potential. I will make a confident decision on how much I want to reach in additional revenue.*

☐ *I will use a planner and a calendar to write my five-year income goal and the action steps to achieve that goal.*

Conclusion

If we want to generate more money, there are many ways we can do so. We need to look at the costs versus the benefits and how our decisions will impact us years from now. Sometimes, our self-doubt and negative mindset get in our way of achieving success in generating more income. We tell ourselves we do not deserve a promotion or a leadership role. We convince ourselves that we are comfortable and should just be satisfied with our current role, even though it is not helping us achieve financial success. We need to shift our thinking and develop enough self-confidence to believe in our abilities. Only then can we realize our potential in life to earn more income and realize our potential!

We must have an organized system for setting an income goal, whether short-term or long-term. Saying we want an additional $5,000 in savings in the next 12 months is a good goal if it is realistic and reasonable. However, there needs to be a system with specific steps to tell us what we will do to get to that goal at the end of the 12 months. That is where the organizational skills come into play. Once we have the organization with finances and income goals set, we can monitor periodically to meet our goals efficiently.

Chapter 6
Saving Money

Can a person make $450,000 a year in income and still be broke? Yes, he can if he is spending over $450,000 each year. We can strive to make more money, but not if our spending surpasses our income. The best approach to not overspending is to save money and not pay for things wastefully. Saving money has many benefits, including:

- Less stress

- More financial independence

- Have money for large, upcoming projects and purchases

- Peace-of-mind

- Financial security

Saving money is just as important as earning money and must be approached in an organized, systematic, and efficient way. The first step to saving is figuring out where the income is going (what we are spending on).

Where is the Money Going?

Unless we figure out where the money is going, we cannot control it and find ways to save. The best thing to do is to calculate percentages and find ways to reduce those percentages. Here are the steps to take:

1) Look at the total set revenues each month, meaning constant money. Some people have varying income because some months they earn more and some months they earn less. Find, on average, how much money comes in each month. Instead of using gross income, use net income. The net income represents the actual money coming in each month minus taxes; therefore, it is a better indicator of revenue.

2) For one month, keep track of daily receipts. Every time a payment is made, a check is written, a good or service is purchased, keep the receipts.

3) Add receipts using Excel or a simple notebook, pencil, and calculator.

4) Calculate percentages of each expense (part to a whole). Here is an example:

Income is $7,256.24.

The mortgage (including taxes and insurance) adds up to $2,679.49.

Calculate the percentage like this:

$$\frac{2679.49}{7256.24} = 0.3693$$

Moving the decimal two places to the right gives us approximately 37%. This means the total percentage spent on rent, insurance, and property taxes adds up to 37%.

Calculate the percentages for all other expenses.

5) Do a Google search to see if the percentages are consistent with what everyone else is paying. For example, on average, people in the United States spend 28% of their gross income on mortgages, including tax, interest, insurance, and principal (Chase, 2021). If our percentage is higher, we need to find ways to reduce the amount. Perhaps we can reduce the insurance costs by shopping around for lower rates.

Some people find that they are drowning in their monthly expenses, and their mortgage payment is up to 60% of their monthly income. The percentage is so outrageous that they must move to a smaller home or a different neighborhood that is more affordable based on their income.

Controlling Debt & Expenses

According to Valuepenguin.com, the top two percentages that Americans spend most of their income is on housing and transportation (2021). A figure shows a breakdown based on 2013 Bureau of Labor Statistics.

Figure 20: Average Household Expenses

Expenditure	Percentage of Budget
Housing	16%
Transportation	14%
Taxes	12%
Utilities & Other Household Operating	11%
Food	10%
Social Security, Pension, Personal Insurance, & IRA Contributions	9%
Debt Payments or Savings	8%
Healthcare	6%
Entertainment	4%
Cash Contributions	3%
Apparel & Related Services	3%
Education	2%
Vices	1%
Miscellaneous	1%
Personal Care	1%
TOTAL	100%

To control expenses effectively and save money, we need to calculate our percentages and find ways to save money in some areas to spend on others. For example, to save money for educational purposes, we need to reduce the percentage in other areas, such as apparel, utilities, travel, etc. Here is an example: If a person earns $86,000 per year and wants to save $6,000 in one year to go on a weeklong trip to Bora Bora, she must save $500 per month for 12 months. She can try to earn more money by doing a side job or getting a second job. She can also try to save the $500 from her monthly spending to save enough for the trip. If she spends $125 on clothes and shoes each month, she must cut this expense entirely or almost completely for one year. Trips to restaurants and dining out can be cut entirely or reduced from 4 visits a month to only 1.

People prioritize their expenses far more effectively when they have strong financial goals, especially savings goals. To have a solid financial plan, we need to know the exact amount to save and by when. Having that deadline and having a total amount helps us figure out what needs to be cut monthly or weekly on some expenses to save for others. Here are some examples of solid financial goals:

- I will pay off my $1,265 balance on my credit card within 15 months.

- I will limit my Christmas gift buying to only $700 this year.

- I will save $1,200 for emergencies within 24 months.

Managing Debt

As mentioned earlier, we accumulate debt when we cannot pay for goods and services upfront. We borrow money. We need to purchase a new computer; we use a credit card. We need to buy a new car; we finance it. We want to purchase beautiful pieces of jewelry and fine shoes. We purchase and pay with a charge card. When we get into debt, it ties up our future income. Even if we want to spend more on certain things, we cannot. Part of our income is already spoken for and, therefore, cannot be used for any other means.

One lesson we can teach the younger generation is how to control debt and spending because the most complex financial concept to comprehend is how borrowed money affects future earnings. Sometimes we have no choice but to get into debt because it takes too long to save. For example, I have never purchased a car by paying up-front. I have never been able to save $15,000 more for this type of purchase. I finance the vehicle I am buying, but these are some of the steps I take:

- I put as much as possible toward a down payment to reduce the total amount financed.

- I shop around and find out the lowest rates before making a purchase.

- I calculate my monthly payment based on the interest rate and prices of vehicles before going to a dealership.

- I do not necessarily go for the car I want; I go for the car I can afford. For example, if I had it my way, I would be driving a Lexus SUV right now. Instead, I am driving a Toyota RAV4 because that's what I can afford based on my budget.

- I stay away from leasing for personal vehicle purchases. When I make a purchase, I get done making the payments in 5 years or less. When I lease, I make payments for three years, then end up financing the car for another 3 to 5 years. If I had made some larger payments and purchased the car, I would have saved time and money in the long run.

If we ask any young, inexperienced person about cars, they likely state they want to purchase a brand-new Mustang, a BMW, or some type of sports car. These are unreasonable choices if they are making minimum wage at their jobs while attending school. They are tying up their future earnings on this significant purchase they cannot afford. As reasonable, experienced adults in their lives, it is up to us to teach them these financial values so they can grow and prosper. We can show them the right path to financial health by showing them how debt and expenses must be controlled over time.

Saving Money with Caution

The one piece of advice I have for saving money is to be careful with losing value. How much are we compromising when we try to save? If we save money on cereal, for example, are we buying a box that is about to expire? Are we compromising reliability if we try to buy a used car with lots of miles? If we buy cheap insurance, are we giving up on great coverage? People often compromise value for savings, which ends up hurting them in the long run. Here are some examples:

- I had a friend in Corona, California, who paid someone $1,200 and promised to redo her kitchen. She gave the money in cash and could not find him after that transaction. Because he was uninsured and unlicensed, she had no recourse and no way to locate him. She decided to go with an unlicensed and uninsured person to save money, which ended up costing her more in the long run.

- To save money, we knew someone who purchased the cheapest possible home insurance policy he could find. When he experienced significant water damage, he realized he had no coverage in the policy against it. Not having proper insurance put him in tremendous debt because he had to end up paying for the loss himself.

- Unfortunately, when it comes to food purchases, people are very inexperienced and ignorant about what to purchase to eat and what to avoid eating. To save money, people buy low-quality foods from local markets that may be cheap but bad for the body.

We must be cautious concerning the value of things we try to save money on. Sometimes, it is better to pay a little more, have peace of mind, and get a good deal from a product or service than go with an option that will give us more stress and problems down the road.

Ideas on How to Save

There are ways to save money on a weekly and monthly basis. To understand saving we must understand spending. There are two types of spending: discretionary and mandatory (Upatanangle.com, 2021). Discretionary spending is variable, like home décor, travel, vacations, clothes, etc. Mandatory spending is on essentials, or fixed bills, like rent, mortgage, etc. Both discretionary and mandatory spending can be reduced or minimized.

Here are 30 ideas on how to save money:

1) Do not purchase to keep a lot of things around the house. Consider becoming a minimalist. The more stuff we have, the more money it will take to store, clean, and preserve. Only buy what we need, except for a few extras like toilet paper, paper towels, staple foods, etc.

2) When shopping around, get three quotes for significant purchases to ensure the price is reasonable for the best value.

3) Have appropriate insurance coverages, including coverage for contents within a home, life insurance, earthquake insurance, etc.

4) Keep telephone bills low by paying off cellular telephones immediately. We can save as much as $50 from a telephone bill just by having paid off phones! There is no need to have the latest and greatest telephone if the one being used works.

5) If monthly revenues have reduced due to unusual circumstances, be sure to downsize to a smaller or more affordable home. It may not be something we want to do but need to do.

6) To avoid late fees, pay bills two months in advance. By doing so, in case we are late or miss a payment, there will not be a penalty.

7) Stop buying coffee & latte from coffee shops. Purchase only once a week or even once a month! Doing so will help cut expenses tremendously. Make coffee and drinks at home and make the run to the coffee shop only as a reward.

8) Set a limit on how much money is going toward lottery tickets.

9) Do not pay extra for online shipping to have it delivered the next day unless we absolutely need it. Use the free shipping method instead.

10) Consider going to a secondhand store to purchase a home, office decorations, or kitchenware.

11) Ask friends and family members for used items we may need, like sofas, refrigerators, desks, chairs, etc. Do not purchase unless it is a last resort.

12) Looking through to find coupons can be beneficial but time-consuming. If time allows, find coupons for things we need before going to the store.

13) Have lists ready, like Target, local grocery store, sporting goods store, before going shopping. It is better to go when multiple items are purchased to save time and gas money.

14) Set a strict budget for food each week and stick to it. For example, buy lunch only once each week. Buy dinner from take-out restaurants only once a week. Cooking at home may be more time-consuming, but definitely, a money-saver.

15) When buying clothes, make sure they can be washed easily using a washer and dryer. If clothes we purchase require dry cleaning, we will spend more money.

16) At restaurants, do not buy drinks. Instead, drink water. Restaurants charge quite a bit of money on drinks, but we can save hundreds of dollars each year by skipping drinks. This is even more important for alcoholic beverages. The cocktails might be enticing but saving money is more important when achieving financial goals.

17) Stock up on items immediately after a holiday to save for next year, like Halloween and Christmas items.

18) Purchase items at the end of a season for most savings. For example, purchase swimsuits in either August or September when the season is about to change. Purchase computers and office supplies in May or June when the school year ends.

19) Use the thermostat wisely. Turn on the air only on hot days when breathing is unbearable. In other words, give up a little comfort to save money and energy.

20) When money is tight, put small gifts together for friends and family members rather than purchasing gift cards and expensive gifts. They will appreciate the effort and understand that some years are more challenging than others.

21) Do as much of our own personal and home maintenance as possible. Put our own nail polish instead of going to a nail salon. Watch Youtube videos to learn how to style and dye our own hair instead of going to a salon. Remove our own weeds in the yard instead of hiring a gardener. Do our own home cleaning instead of hiring a cleaning crew.

22) Make it a habit to question ourselves every time we take out our wallet to pay for something whether the purchase is essential. For example, is it necessary to buy popcorn and soda at the movies, or can we do without? Is it necessary to take our car to a car wash every month? Is it essential to purchase another pair of shoes – is it necessary to do so, or is it just nice to have? Question every purchase!

23) Either stop purchasing sodas, cigarettes, packaged salads, precut foods, massages, and other discretionary items or curtail them.

24) Use a bank that does not charge too many fees, like a credit union! In addition, use direct deposit as often as possible.

25) To stay motivated to save, use a buddy system or purchase used books on money-saving habits. Having a "buddy," like a self-help book, will help hold each other accountable.

Reading a book on saving and personal finances will support our focus on our financial goals.

26) Buy clothes only to replace items that have been ruined or destroyed.

27) Save coins and change in a container. Once a year, take the total accumulated and use it toward a financial goal.

28) Write a meal plan for the entire week. Then, write the ingredients needed based on breakfast, lunch, and dinner plans each day of the week. Go shopping using the ingredient list to save time and money.

Figure 21: Weekly Meal Plan

Weekly Meal Plan	
Monday	
Breakfast	
Lunch	
Dinner	
Tuesday	
Breakfast	
Lunch	
Dinner	
Wednesday	
Breakfast	
Lunch	
Dinner	
Thursday	
Breakfast	
Lunch	
Dinner	
Friday	
Breakfast	
Lunch	
Dinner	
Saturday	
Breakfast	
Lunch	
Dinner	

Sunday	
Breakfast	
Lunch	
Dinner	

Figure 22: Grocery Store List

Grocery Store List			
Meat/Seafood		Frozen Items	
Fruits/Vegetables		Baking Goods	
Drinks/Wine/Spirits		Deli	

Downloadable versions of these two items are available at Efficiencyandorganization.com/products.

29) When cooking or baking, do not get rare ingredients; we will only use them once or twice. Use ingredients that we will use over and over again.

30) Save water as much as possible by repairing leaky faucets, cutting back on shower time, watching how much water goes toward washing dishes, and how often the lawn gets watered. Use the washer and dryer only if enough clothes cover at least half of the load.

Saving money could mean depriving ourselves of certain pleasures in life. This depravity makes people not want to save when they really should. Especially in this day in age when everything is about instant gratification, it could be hard to say "no" to self sometimes. The best way to combat the negative feelings associated with depravity is to trick the mind by playing a game. We will call it the money-saving game! When we play the game, and each time we save, we win, or we score. The financial goal is the obstacle, and each time we save, we get closer to overcoming the obstacle, just like in games!

Paying for Services vs. Doing Them Ourselves

We can outsource a variety of activites and chores. We can hire people to do all kinds of things for us, including:

- Cutting the grass

- Cleaning our house, including laundry, dishes, etc.

- Driving kids to and from school

- Bookkeeping/paying bills

- Washing car

- Party-planning

- Hiring nannies to watch the kids

- Hiring a cook for our meals

Paying others to do services that we do not want, like cleaning the home, is convenient. If saving money is a big financial goal, we must curtail some of this spending. We must consider doing as many chores and activities for ourselves instead of outsourcing. With proper time management, self-motivation, self-discipline, and organization, we can get it all done ourselves and meet our financial goals.

There is also the idea of doing things ourselves (instead of having others do them for us) to help us stay grounded and humble. We would think that celebrities hire people to do everything for them, but that's just not the case. Even wealthy and successful people, like Mark Cuban, have admitted to doing things around their homes because they like the experience of doing things themselves.

Some things we simply cannot do ourselves. For example, most people cannot fix the engine of a car, cut branches off of trees, or do alterations to clothes. If it is absolutely necessary to outsource, we should.

Strategies, Ideas, and Steps to Improving Personal Finances

Here are some strategies and ideas to keep us all on track with better money management based on this chapter. Planning and organizing will set us on the right path to success with our financial goals. All actions and steps shown in each chapter can be found in Chapter 9 accumulated altogether.

- *Calculate the percentages you spend each month of your gross income on various expenses to see how they compare to other averages.*

- *Think carefully about making any purchase that will put you into debt. Figure out how soon you can pay the debt to free up your money.*

- *Have a specific financial goal with a definite amount and a deadline. Doing this will help you work toward a goal and keep you motivated to save, save, save! Here are two examples: I will save $5,000 in one year. I will pay off $3,400 in debt in one year.*

- *Write down the financial goal and put it somewhere visible so you can hold yourself accountable for achieving it.*

- *Make a list of 10 ways you are willing to save money each week on discretionary and mandatory expenses. Stick to it by reminding yourself daily that you need to meet your financial goal and cannot waver from these new money-saving habits!*

Conclusion

As with many adults who make middle-income wages, it is hard to save money because they make very little and live in an area where the cost of living is high. All the money they earn goes towards bills, and there is almost no disposable income for fun spending. If they want to buy things they cannot afford, they must take out loans or credit cards. The problem with those is high-interest rates. Therefore, planning and doing some organized savings can help avoid getting things that will cost more money because of interest.

There are various advantages to saving money, including:

- Reaching financial goals

- Having enough money set aside for emergencies and unexpected expenses

- Having money for large purchases

- Peace of mind

- Less stress and anxiety

- Setting a good example

- Legacy (passing money to other generations)

The first step in saving is figuring out where money is going. The second step is looking at each spending category to decide what cuts to make. The third step is coming up with a precise financial goal so there is a reason to save. The purpose must be specific (have a set value) and have a deadline. By doing this, we are playing a game with ourselves to see how quickly and efficiently we can get to that goal in an organized system. The fourth step involves saving. We can use a variety of ways to save until we meet the financial goal, which involves saving, or paying off debt.

This book focuses on the organizational and planning process of personal finances. To learn more about money, personal finances, investments, and money-saving strategies, please consider reading some of the books and blogs of experts. Here is a list of professionals who offer advice, ideas, and resources in their books and blogs on personal finances. We can pass what we learn from these individuals to friends, neighbors, and kids in our families to help set them on the right path to financial success!

LEARN MORE ABOUT PERSONAL FINANCES

From these authors

Dave Ramsey

Book: Dave Ramsey's Complete Guide to Money

Suze Orman

Book: The Money Book for the Young, Fabulous, and Broke

Robert Kiyosaki

Book: Rich Dad, Poor Dad

Cary Siegel

Why Didn't They Teach Me This in School? 99 Personal Money Management Principles to Live By

Vicki Robin

Your Money or Your Life

Rachel Cruze

Book: Love Your Life Not Theirs

efficiencyandorganization.com

Chapter 7
Being Prepared for Emergencies and the Unexpected

One of the most profound lessons I have learned over the years has been being prepared for emergencies and unexpected circumstances that suddenly arise. Sometimes, no matter how much we plan, unforeseen things do happen. Those events could affect our finances negatively. Here is a small list of things that could occur:

- Car repairs

- Earthquakes and natural disasters

- Home repairs

- Unexpected travel expenses

- Deaths in the family

- Medical emergencies

- Family issues

- Technology issues

- Job loss

If the car suddenly would not start, we need money to have it towed to a mechanic. The estimated repairs could be $1,200 or more. Would we be able to pay for them? Do we have money saved up for that unexpected expense? Many of us do not have enough saved for unforeseen expenses arising in our everyday life. In fact, 27% of Americans report that if an emergency occurs where they have to come up with $400 or more, they would have to sell something to get the funds needed (CNBC.com, 2019). According to the Federal Reserve, "Nearly 3 in 10 adults were either unable to pay their monthly bills or were one modest financial setback away from failing to pay monthly bills in full (Federalreserve.gov, 2020).

Millions of people are unprepared for emergencies, and those emergencies and unexpected expenses could send them into poverty. The biggest culprit is a medical emergency. If someone is underinsured or not insured and breaks a bone, the hospital bills can rack up quickly. He could suddenly find himself in tens of thousands of dollars in debt.

A person could be let go from a job due to significant layoffs. If she cannot find employment within a few months, she can go from earning a middle-class income to living in poverty.

Emergencies and unexpected circumstances are real things affecting millions of people worldwide. The best approach to handling emergencies is financial preparedness. Here are some ways in which individuals can deal with emergencies and the unexpected to survive a financial crisis: Insurance, credit cards, and other means. Each of these is discussed in this chapter.

Insurance

Insurance and peace-of-mind fit together so mutually and conformingly. The entire concept of insurance rests on the idea of having protection in case of unforeseen or unexpected circumstances or emergencies. Depending on the type of coverage, having proper insurance with a reputable company can make a huge difference in people's lives. People who have acquired a large amount of wealth have plenty of insurance protection in place. They are covered for almost every aspect of life! It could be for

- Home insurance

- Auto insurance

- Life insurance

- Health insurance

- Rental insurance

- Earthquake insurance

- Business owner insurance

- Flood insurance

- Boat/RV/Motorcycle

Figure 23: Common Types of Personal Insurance Policies

The most common policies are auto and home insurance since most people own cars and homes. Imagine this scenario: We are a tenant in an apartment building. There is a massive fire that takes place. All our belongings burn in the fire. We get some money from the landlords and their insurance company for moving expenses to live elsewhere but are told there is no coverage in their policy for our contents. In other words, they will not give any money to replace the items tenants lost in the fire because it was their responsibility to provide that protection. The leasing contract we signed may have stated that we were responsible for purchasing our own rental insurance policy. Do we have $10,000, $15,000, $20,000, or more to replace all the items lost in the fire? We will be okay if we have that money in an emergency savings account.

However, most people do. If there were insurance in place, our out-of-pocket cost would have been about $500, which is a typical policy deductible amount, and the insurance company would have taken care of the rest.

The concept is the same for auto insurance. I run into so many young people who think they just can't catch a break! When they feel they are making a little bit of headway in life, financially speaking, a disaster happens, and they fall right back where they were. For example, their laptop gets taken from their car, and their car gets stolen. Now, they are without a computer or a car. They have an accident and cannot pay to repair or replace their vehicle. A tree falls on their car, and other such scenarios set them back financially. These are typical setbacks that can and do take place. They would have been protected if they had paid for insurance coverage that included comprehensive and collision coverage for their vehicle. Yes, they would have spent a few hundred dollars extra each year. Still, they would have had protection to replace lost, stolen, or damaged items!

"When you have insurance you know that you are secured against any unforeseen events in life, and this gives you complete peace of mind." – IFFCO Tokio

Most people understand the concept of insurance but do not purchase a policy because they do not like the idea of paying money up front for protection. They figure they are saving money by not paying for protection they may not need. The earlier people understand and embrace the idea of insurance, the more financially secure and stable they will be in the future should disastrous situations occur; catastrophic problems almost always happen at some point in time! Ask young people if they have health insurance in place, and they will likely say they do not unless they are covered by their parents' policy or an employer. They figure, why pay the $100 or so for coverage each month if they are healthy and doubtful that anything should happen to them? But what if something does happen? Is it worth raising medical bills at such a young age and not being able to afford them?

According to Fightbills.com, the top five reasons why people file for bankruptcy include:

- Divorce

- Medical bills

- Mismanagement of loans and debt

- Job loss/reduced income

- Unexpected emergencies

The idea of filing for bankruptcy may sound reasonable, given that a person gets a fresh financial start, but it's not easy or desirable. A person's credit gets ruined due to bankruptcy, and it could take five to ten years to recover and rebuild that credit. With proper insurance in place, monthly or annual policy fees do need to be paid, but at least there will be a peace of mind knowing there is protection in case of an emergency or disaster!

Health Insurance and Life Insurance

Having coverage is incredibly helpful when needed. We often do not see the need for health insurance until something unexpected, like a broken leg, a fractured bone, a bad case of the flu, blood clots, anxiety, disorders, and other health concerns arise. The cheapest policies are the ones with the highest deductibles. Such policies can be purchased as long as we know if we have a $2,500 or a $5,000 deductible, we have that money set aside in case we get billed by the hospital.

Life insurance is very inexpensive to purchase at a young age. A healthy 18-year-old can purchase a policy for $1 million in coverage for $25 per month! The policy will be in effect until she is 95 years old. The sooner a person starts investing in life insurance, the better. Death is inevitable. We do not know when our time on earth will end. We must consider having a policy to protect our family members in case of our untimely death. Why leave them with bills and financial insecurities when we can leave them with money to pay for expenses after death?

Some people are firmly against the concept of life insurance as a matter of principal. Instead of life insurance, they invest in other items that can easily be sold by family members in case they pass away. For example, they invest in properties, mutual funds, bonds, precious metals, etc. They also take care of funeral and other death-related costs through mortuaries and burial grounds, so families do not have to struggle financially to come up with the money when their death.

Home Insurance, Rental Insurance, and Auto Insurance

Besides health and life insurance, most people will probably purchase an auto and a homeowner or rental policy in their lives. Most home insurance policies are comprehensive and have much coverage and protection against disastrous events. Imagine these scenarios:

- Tree falls on the roof

- Thieves enter and take our valuables

- The roots of one of the trees on our property get in the pipes and cause major damage

- The dog runs out the door and bites someone walking in front of the home

Wouldn't it give us peace of mind knowing that we have a policy that would take care of the costs related to these events in case they should take place? That's what home insurance policies do! They help cover costs that are unexpected and sudden.

Rental insurance policies are for renters. Property owners purchase insurance coverage for the main buildings, including windows, roofs, and fences. Their policies do not provide coverage for tenants' personal property. Imagine how much money it would take to replace everything in our apartment units if we had to do it. The furniture in every room, not including all other items, would cost about $5,000 or more to replace. Rental policies are usually inexpensive and provide peace of mind, like all other insurance policies.

If we own a condominium, the policies are similar to rental insurance policies. The associations will cover the main areas, pipes, fences, roofs, windows, etc. Interior walls, ceilings, floors, and personal property get covered by a separate condominium insurance policy that we can purchase.

We are most familiar with auto insurance policies. Depending on the state, the liability insurance requirements differ. For example, in California, we are required to have a liability policy in place if we drive. We are liable if we accidentally cause damage or harm others in an accident that is our fault. However, other coverages could be included in the policy. We could add rental coverage, towing, collision, and comprehensive coverage that provides protection and financial compensation in cases like:

- Stolen vehicle

- Stolen items from the vehicle

- Water damage in the interior

- Falling trees or branches

- Lighting

Collision coverage is mostly to repair our cars if we get into an accident. If I have an accident and it is my fault, my insurance company can pay to fix my car. Even if I get into an accident, that is not my fault, I would still get my car repaired if I have collision coverage.

Other Policies

Besides health, life, home, rental, or car insurance, other policies can be available to purchase. For example, in earthquake-prone areas, there are earthquake insurance policies. If we own expensive jewelry pieces, we can schedule them on our rental or home insurance policies. We can buy a policy for an RV, motorcycle, or boat. Flood insurance is available for areas where homes are too close to water bodies. There are also insurance policies for business owners, like:

- Product liability

- General liability

- Professional liability

- Commercial auto

- Pollution liability

- Inland marine/cargo

- Workers' compensation

- And much more!

Figure 24: Common Types of Business Insurance Policies

Common Types of Business Insurance Policies

·Product liability
·General liability
·Professional liability
·Commercial auto
·Pollution liability
·Inland marine/cargo
·Workers' compensation

Insurance is so critical for financial safety and security that when making large purchases, like boats, homes, recreational vehicles, and starting businesses, most experts immediately look into the cost and availability of insurance. Conversation with an insurance agent or broker can help us understand what policies are available and at what price, depending on our lifestyle or living situation. Getting the information is resourceful and helpful in organizing our financial situation with peace of mind and extra security.

Emergency Savings

Besides insurance, the second-best way to be prepared for emergencies and unexpected occurrences is to have money set aside for emergencies. It takes tremendous discipline to save money and not touch it unless there is an emergency. Sometimes, we tend to save, but use the money for reasons that do not constitute an emergency. I have done that on several occasions due to my lack of self-discipline with money! What constitutes an emergency for me sometimes is not really an emergency. I convince myself that accessing the money is for a good, worthwhile reason and end up spending it.

If we use emergency savings, we must replenish the funds as soon as possible. The best approach is to see that money as debt borrowed against ourselves. If we take out funds from that account, we must have a plan to pay it back right away. Most financial experts agree that having three or six months' worth of savings is the proper approach to emergency savings. For example, if our monthly expenses add up to $2,700, we should have about $8,000 saved for emergencies (based on three months). The amount is slightly more than $16,000 if we save for six months.

Saving $8,000 is challenging. If a third of Americans do not have $400 saved up, imagine how hard it would be to save $8,000 or more – how long it will take and how much effort. Therefore, another approach is to consider the major things that could break or go wrong for which we would need money immediately. Here are some questions to think about:

1) Is my car old enough to where I think I would experience a sudden repair issue that might cost about $2,000? Do I have that money saved somewhere in case of an emergency?

2) Are my home appliances in good shape? How much would I need to have saved if I suddenly had to replace one?

3) If I use my computer at all times and I rely on it, what would it cost to replace it if it were to get damaged?

Having enough just to cover the most important things might require us to save less than three months' worth of salary. The amount could be for $500, $600, $1,000, $2,000, or $2,500. We could take small steps by getting ready for the most immediate situations that might arise. Here are examples:

- Replacing an appliance
- Making necessary repairs
- Purchasing books for school at the start of the semester
- Making an essential purchase for the home
- Travel expenses for the funeral of a loved one who is in the advanced stages of cancer

- Deductibles for a medical treatment

Credit Cards or Personal Loans

If we can pay off a credit card at the end of each month, using it for emergencies may not be such a bad idea! Wewill avoid the finance charges if we pay off the balance, and we can even earn points that can be used for future purchases. The trick, though, is to be able to pay off at the end of the month. If this is not possible, it's best to not use a credit card at all and instead focus on setting some money aside for emergencies in an easy-access savings account.

Personal loans could be challenging to get and take some time to qualify for. Usually, a banking institution would need to run a credit report, do work verification, and look for collateral before issuing a personal loan. If money needs to be accessed right away, a personal loan may not be a viable option. If time is not of immediate essence, a personal loan can help, especially if there is no penalty for paying off early to avoid paying too much in interest!

Whether getting a personal loan or using a credit card, it is important to have a good credit score. A good score will ensure chances of obtaining loans and getting the lowest rates. The rates will dictate how much money gets paid in interest each month. Those interest payments add up! According to Experian, one of the world's leading credit reporting companies, the top 5 factors that affect a score include:

- Credit history length

- Amounts owed

- Payment history

- Number of credit accounts recently opened

- Diversity of portfolio (types of credit accounts that are open)

The more creditors, bankers, and lending institutions trust us, the more money they will be willing to lend, and the faster and the lowest cost (interest charged). To build credit and increase a score, here are some recommendations:

- Track loan and credit card due dates each month. Instead of waiting for the billing notice to arrive, write the dates due in a planner or calendar to ensure paying on time or earlier than due, if possible.

- Pay a little more than the required monthly installment amount to pay off debt quicker and increase FICO score.

- At least once a year, check your credit history to ensure it is accurate.

- Try to be below a 50% debt-to-credit ratio. In other words, if the available credit on a card for $1,000, let's ensure the balance is below $500. In fact, some experts advise that the ratio be less than 30% of allowable credit (Debt.org, 2021).

- We mustn't open too many new accounts simultaneously, as this will hurt our credit score.

- After paying off the debt, let's not close the account. The more versatility there is in our credit history, and the more balanced paid, the more FICO scores will increase.

It is worth looking into other strategies by researching and reading about credit building. The more we know, the more we can work on building credit. A good credit score will allow us to have one or two credit cards on hand in cases of emergency.

Other Means

Some other ways to be prepared for financial emergencies include borrowing from family, getting a payday loan, selling investments, and selling items through a pawn shop or online. Although these may be options, they are not the best-case scenario in many instances.

For example, borrowing from a family member may be viable but embarrassing and humiliating. Also, going to family members repeatedly may lead them to scold us for not managing money properly, causing further embarrassment and disappointment.

A payday loan is an option for most people but not the best option. These are high-cost, short-term loans that must only be accessed if in dire need. For example, under California law, up to $300 can be borrowed (California Dept. of Payday Loans, 2019). Other states, like Idaho and Illinois, allow up to $1,000 to be borrowed (NCSL, 2021). This amount must quickly be paid off upon payday. The fees are high. On a $300 payday loan, we might get charged up to $45. In other words, we are paying an institution $45 just for giving us our earned money a few days before we actually get it in our account! Some people do this with their tax refunds. If they are due back $1,800 from the IRS, for instance, they pay a tax preparer $300 so they can get the money a few days to a week faster than the actual deposit day. As consumers, we must be careful with the fees involved because although it is nice to get the money one or two days faster, we have to consider the fees that will cost us.

Selling investments is an option, but unfortunately, liquidating the money may take a while. For example, we might say we have money in our home equity to cash out. That takes time! It can take at least 15 days to get money out of home equity, and even more if we sell the property. Selling other personal property may also be time-consuming, like a boat, a recreational vehicle, a car, a prized collection, gold, silver, etc. Depending on the time of year and the economy, some items may not have the same value now as they would at other times. For example, when the economy is in a recession, gold sells at a high price. However, stock prices are generally along with home values. We might face lower or higher offers for the items we own depending on when we try to sell and what we try to sell.

Pawn shops may not offer as much as our items are worth if we try to sell things through them. The same could be said for selling online. Values of things are so subjective that what one person may think is worth a certain amount may not be the same as another. For example, I took a ring I wanted to sell to a pawn shop seven years ago. One place offered to buy it from me for $80, while another offered over $300!

Strategies, Ideas, and Steps to Improving Personal Finances

Planning and organizing will set us on the right path to success with our financial goals. Based on what has been shared in this chapter, some strategies and ideas can help keep us all on track with better money management. All actions and steps shown in each chapter can be found in Chapter 9 accumulated altogether.

- ☐ *Check your credit history within the next two weeks to look for inaccuracies and to verify your credit score.*

- ☐ *Research online monthly to learn how to improve my credit score for the next six months. The more you know, the more you will be empowered!*

- ☐ *Make an appointment with your insurance broker to determine if you have adequate coverage for various insurance needs.*

- ☐ *Do a calculation to see how much money you would need to have saved for emergencies based on your income and job security.*

Conclusion

Financial safety nets are of utmost importance for people with a middle-class income. Disasters and unfortunate events are part of life. They take place unexpectedly and with no warning. There are steps to become financially organized and efficient by having appropriate insurance policies, an emergency savings account, and a couple of other financial safeguards to help us stand back up after an unexpected fall.

Chapter 8
Organized System for Financial Goal Setting

There is a famous quote by Lewis Carroll, the author of Alice in Wonderland, that goes, "If you don't know where you are going, any road will get you there." Goals represent the "where," while the "roads" represent the action plans we take to get to those destinations. Goals can be related to our personal lives, careers, educational endeavors, finances, etc. Goals are essential when it comes to managing personal finances as middle-class wage earners.

One process to follow when attempting to set and achieve short-term or long-term goals is first to visualize what it would be like to achieve success. That vision of being successful will help us stay on track to achieve them in a given time. The second step is to write out a goal like a SMART goal. In other words, it has to be specific, attainable, and timely. The third part is to have action plans that are specific enough to help us work toward achievement. Fourth is tracking or monitoring our progress along the way. The last step in the process is celebration the accomplishment at the very end!

Goal Achievement Process

Formulate your vision of success: How does it feel achieving success with what you want to achieve?

Write specific action plans that must be completed with deadlines in order to achieve the overarching goal.

Celebrate your success and move on to a new goal!!!

Write a SMART goal: It needs to be realistic, attainable, measurable, and timely.

Monitor your progress every week, every 2 weeks, or every month.

An efficient and organized process

Here are examples of goals that people can set for the various aspects of their lives:

Personal/Health: I will lose 20 pounds in 90 days.

Professional: I will get a promotion at work within the next 18 months.

Educational: I will take a class on digital media for one semester at the community college and complete it with an A or a B.

Family: We will go on a family vacation within the next 12 months to enjoy our time together.

Personal Development: I will read six self-help books in the next nine months.

With each of these goals, we can visualize success when we accomplish our goals. For example, we can imagine ourselves looking in the mirror in 3 months and seeing ourselves less heavy by 20 pounds. We can see ourselves working at our newly promoted job. We can see ourselves with the family on a trip somewhere. The vision is important, because that will be the motivating factor to keep us going and achieving.

The next steps in the process for each of these would be to devise action plans that we can monitor daily, weekly, biweekly, or monthly until the goals are realized. Financial goals are no different. They need to be set with a vision in mind for success, be specific, timely, and have action plans that can be monitored.

Setting Short-Term Goals

Short-term financial goals are those we set to accomplish in less than 12 months. Here are some examples:

- I will save $500 for emergency funds in the next 12 months.

- I will pay off $360 in credit card debt between now and six months.

- My family and I will go on a short vacation within the next year, costing us less than $2,000.

- We will replace our kitchen appliances for less than $2,000 between now and June.

- I will have two-yard sales in the next 12 months and raise $500 from them combined.

Setting Long-Term Goals

Long-term financial goals take more than 12 months to achieve. Here are some examples:

- Between now and two years from now, I will save enough money to upgrade 2 of the bathrooms in my home.

- I will pay off $6,000 within the next 18 months.

- I will start an investment plan involving putting $100 monthly in stocks and mutual funds.

- I will cut my total credit card debt to $2,000 within the next two years or less.

- I will save $20,000 within the next four years to be able to purchase a home.

Action Plans

Once the goals are set, the next step involves writing some specific action plans, in nature. Unless we are specific with the things we are going to do to achieve success, it's going to be difficult, or almost impossible, to realize our goals. Let's say we select a goal to pay off $4,000 in debt in one year. What are some ways we can make that goal happen? Here are sample action plans:

- No buying lunch or breakfast (taking food from home for lunch and breakfast each day)

- No buying clothes, shoes, or accessories for one year

- No vacations for one year

- Eating food from restaurants only once each week (cooking at home mostly)

- Getting rid of monthly subscriptions

- Doing own manicures, pedicures, etc. instead of going to salons

- Save $50 or more on groceries each week by cutting on non-essential food items

- Stop buying alcohol and cigarettes

- Selling items that are no longer needed

- Cutting cable

    For more resources on how to save money each day, visit the following sources on Pinterest.com:

- *80 Ways to Live a Frugal Life (Tips on How to Be Frugal)*

- *How to Live Cheap: 32 (easy) Cheap Living Tips*

- *30 Easy Ways to Reduce Household Expenses and Save Hundreds*

Research other ideas for saving money on Google or other search engines by typing "money-saving ideas" or other related phrases.

Examples of Short-Term and Long-Term Financial SMART Goals

1. I will buy food from restaurants just once a week and cook the rest of my meals.

2. I will drink water instead of soda or other drinks that cost more money.

3. I will recycle all cans and bottles and turn them in for money.

4. I will look at my balances in accounts every other day to track where money is going.

5. I will sell items I not use on apps, such as decorative items, kitchen items, electric tools, etc., within the next three months.

6. I will work out at home instead of a gym membership.

7. I will check out books from the library or buy used ones.

8. I will call cable company, phone company, etc., and possibly switch to another carrier to save more money.

9. I will look at the thermostat - lower or higher the temperature to save money on warm or cold days.

10. I will cut the number of trips I take to Starbucks by 75%.

11. I will check out thrift shops first before going to the mall.

12. I will ask friends and family if they have things they can give me rather than making a purchase.

13. I will shop around for lower insurance rates within the next three months.

14. I will pay off all my credit card debt to save money on interest within three years.

15. I will cut my cable bill within two months.

16. If my bank charges fees, I will switch to a credit union!

17. I will buy only things essential for the home, me, and the family.

18. I will turn off appliances when they are not used to save money on electric bills.

19. I will be careful with how much I spend on alcohol and tobacco products (cut by 75%).

20. I will research ways to save money through Google, Pinterest, and other sites.

21. I will buy more chicken instead of beef - it costs less.

22. I will not upgrade to a new phone if it's unnecessary to save on our phone bills.

23. I will cut all memberships and subscriptions I do not use.

24. I will declutter and organize our home within three months so I know what items I have and not waste money on duplicates.

25. I will cut water usage each month, even if it means shorter shower times.

Monitoring Goals

Once goals and action plans are written down (and they should be written down), there needs to be careful monitoring taking place. Monitoring means checking on progress to keep oneself accountable. We can check on our progress weekly, biweekly, monthly, or quarterly for the best results. Suppose we have a financial goal set with 3 to 5 specific action plans. We can set a biweekly reminder in our calendar (paper or electronic) to review how we are doing and hold ourselves accountable. If one of the action plans was only to cook food at home and not eat from outside restaurants for three months, are we on track? Are we actually sticking with the action plan and the goal? If so, great! If not, we know we must change routines and habits to make that action plan a reality.

Monitoring goals is one of the most critical ways to help achieve any goal. People can set all their goals, especially at the beginning of a year. Without following through and monitoring themselves through self-discipline, goal achievement will not occur.

What happens if, through the monitoring process, we find that we are sticking to our action plans? We should celebrate! The celebration can be a simple gesture – something we give ourselves as an extra incentive – to give yourself credit for our hard work and dedication to achieving the goal. Celebrating ideas include:

- Cooking an extra special meal, like lobster, for dinner

- Spending an afternoon lounging around the backyard or pool area

- Taking a drive out to a nearby beach or lake

- Buying oneself a sweater or a summer top from a local clothing store

Strategies, Ideas, and Steps to Improving Personal Finances

Planning and organizing will set us on the right path to success with our financial goals. Based on what has been shared in this chapter, some strategies and ideas can help keep us all on track with better money management. All actions and steps shown in each chapter can be found in Chapter 9 accumulated altogether.

☐ *Develop 1 to 3 short-term financial goals and specific action plans for each.*

☐ *Create 1 to 3 long-term financial goals and specific action plans for each.*

☐ *Write down how often to check on progress with goals or how often to monitor progress.*

☐ *Celebrate successes after accomplishing and achieving financial goals.*

Chapter 9
Combined List of Strategies, Ideas, and Steps: A Checklist

The strategies, ideas, and steps compiled from all chapters are combined into one chapter here. This compiled list can serve as a checklist to put strategies into actions immediately.

Chapter 1 Steps and Strategies

- ☐ *Write a goal to organize your finances immediately. Here is an example: I will start using a monthly system to know exactly how much I am earning and how much I can afford to spend.*

- ☐ *Take about two hours to sit down and log into my checking account online.*

- ☐ *If the amount of money spent (going out) is more than the amount earned (coming in), focus on two things:*

  - ○ *How can you generate more money? Can you get a promotion? Can you improve your skills to get a promotion? Can you start a side business that will generate more income immediately? Can you change jobs?*

  - ○ *How can you spend less money? Can you take each item on my spending list and see if there is a way to reduce or eliminate it?*

- ☐ *Calendar a time each week or month to sit down (preferably on the weekend) for a 2-hour or 3-hour period to calculate money coming in and money going out (personal budget.*

- ☐ *Figure out which calculator you like the most; either the computer calculator, a phone, or an actual calculator purchased from an office supply store.*

- ☐ *Based on some reasons why people have difficulty with personal money management listed in chapter 1, pick which one(s) resonate(s) with me, if any. Figuring out the root cause will help me determine what you need to work on fixing.*

Chapter 2 Steps and Strategies

☐ *If I am in debt, I will put together a document together showing how much I owe and how much I am spending paying off debt each month.*

☐ *If I have small credit card balances, I will focus on paying them off one by one. I will make smaller payments on the more significant card balances until I pay off the smaller ones.*

☐ *To pay off debt, I will look at every item I pay money for each month and adjust. The money I save on other things will go directly into paying the debt. For example, if I reduce my cable bill by $23.00, I will ensure that $23.00 goes directly toward a credit card balance.*

☐ *I will not completely cut off all enjoyments I get out of life to pay off debt because complete depravity is not the way to go. I will, however, curtain some actions and activities. For example, instead of getting a Frappuccino every other day, I will only get one per week, or better yet, one every two weeks.*

☐ *I will try to change my debt balances to a credit card with a much lower interest rate or negotiate with the existing credit card company to reduce the rate as much as possible.*

☐ *When I get a more considerable sum of money at once, like tax returns or birthday gifts, I will pay most of it toward debt.*

☐ *I will give myself a small celebration as I pay off each credit card debt. For example, I can get a small dessert from somewhere to enjoy, get a pedicure, or go to the beach for a day.*

☐ *I will use an Excel sheet to keep all finances organized or paper forms. There are debt trackers and personal financial templates that are helpful and useful if I research to* *find them. We can even purchase them for $1.00 or $2.00 on efficiencyandorganization.com/products.*

☐ *I will teach my children, grandchildren, nieces, or nephews about money matters. I will ask them what they know about debt, income, expenses, etc. I will help them figure out how they can learn more about personal finances.*

☐ *I will research once a month to learn about debt-reducing strategies.*

☐ *I will have 3 specific goals that I track each month for my personal financial success. Here are examples:*

> *I will save $1,600 to get two doors replaced in my home within one year.*
>
> *I will put a limit and spend no more than $600 on clothes and shoes in the next 12 months.*
>
> *I will take a free or low-fee college class to acquire more skills and knowledge to help me get a promotion and earn more money within the next two years.*

Chapter 3 Steps and Strategies

☐ *Use a T-chart to determine past financial decisions and actions that are positive and negative.*

☐ *Use a debt tracker to determine how much is owed for various debts and loans and what the monthly interest amounts paid are.*

☐ *Give yourself a financial questionnaire to determine what you want to work on immediately to improve your financial situation.*

☐ *Set 3 to 5 financial goals based on examples in Figure 8 that involve a time factor and are specific in nature.*

☐ *Set specific action plans for each of the goals.*

☐ *Set monitoring frequency to know when to revisit the goal and check off the associated action plans.*

☐ *Choose a few organizational tips to implement to stay decluttered, neat, coordinated, and structured with personal finances.*

☐ *Organize personal finances by filing money-related documents sorted and filed or saved in files on the computer.*

☐ *Declutter and throw out old money-related paperwork once a week, month, or year, or scan and save in folders on the computer or USB drive.*

☐ *If doing the financial organization is too stressful a task, hire a bookkeeper to do this for you each month.*

Chapter 4 Steps and Strategies

☐ *Make a two-column budget for yourself or download one that you can use every week to calculate income and expenses.*

☐ *On the first of each month, write in your planner or calendar that you must create the budget with expected income and expenses for that month.*

☐ *For the income column, on the first of the month, write down the exact amounts you expect to get in the form of income that month and estimated amounts (if any).*

☐ *For the expense column, on the first of the month, write down the exact amounts and estimated amounts for each type of expense you will have that month.*

☐ *Make sure you account for how much you expect or plan on saving that month when you set up your budget for the first month.*

☐ *Look at every one of the expenses and see how you can cut costs, if at all. Then, make calls or go online to figure out what you need to do to make those savings immediately.*

☐ *Select a specific day of the week to review the budget – income versus expenses. Selecting a particular day and even an exact time of day will increase organization and consistency.*

Chapter 5 Steps and Strategies

☐ *If I receive unexpected funds, I will either save, pay off debt, or use it for something important, like home repairs, car repairs, going into a certification program, etc.*

☐ *I will read a book this year that can help me shift from having a negative mindset to having more confidence in myself to earn more money and increase my income.*

☐ *I will review my insurance policies within two months to ensure I am adequately covered. I will contact my insurance broker for advice.*

☐ *In the next three months, I will carefully consider ways to generate or earn more income to realize my full financial potential. I will make a confident decision on how much I want to earn in additional revenue.*

☐ *I will use a planner and a calendar to write my five-year income goal and the action steps to achieve that goal.*

Chapter 6 Steps and Strategies

☐ *Calculate the percentages you spend each month of your gross income on various expenses to see how they compare to other averages.*

☐ *Think carefully about making any purchase that will put you into debt. Figure out how soon you can pay the debt to free up your money.*

☐ *Have a specific financial goal with a definite amount and a deadline. Doing this will help you work toward a goal and keep you motivated to save, save, save! Here are two examples: I will save $5,000 in one year. I will pay off $3,400 in debt in one year.*

☐ *Write down the financial goal and put it somewhere visible so you can hold yourself accountable for achieving it.*

☐ *Make a list of 10 ways you are willing to save money each week on discretionary and mandatory expenses. Stick to it by reminding yourself daily that you need to meet your financial goal and cannot waver from these new money-saving habits!*

Chapter 7 Steps and Strategies

☐ *Check your credit history within the next two weeks to look for inaccuracies and to verify your credit score.*

☐ *Research online monthly to learn how to improve my credit score for the next six months. The more you know, the more you will be empowered!*

☐ *Make an appointment with your insurance broker to determine if you have adequate coverage for various insurance needs.*

☐ *Do a calculation to see how much money you would need to have saved for emergencies based on your income and job security.*

Chapter 8 Steps and Strategies

☐ *Come up with 1 to 3 short-term financial goals along with specific action plans for each.*

☐ *Come up with 1 to 3 long-term financial goals along with specific action plans for each.*

☐ *Write down how often you will check on your progress with your goals, or how often you will monitor your progress.*

Chapter 9 Steps and Strategies

☐ *Develop 1 to 3 short-term financial goals and specific action plans for each.*

☐ *Create 1 to 3 long-term financial goals and specific action plans for each.*

☐ *Write down how often to check on progress with goals or how often to monitor progress.*

☐ *Celebrate successes after accomplishing and achieving financial goals.*

Conclusion

Many of the books on personal finances that are currently on the market focus on getting rich quickly. They all claim to have the formula for becoming wealthy quickly if the readers follow their plans. Most Americans, however, want financial freedom and simply to have enough to live comfortably. Their desire is not to become filthy rich. They want to be able to afford the home they want, save enough money for their children's college education, travel a few times a year, have retirement money set aside, and live comfortably.

Getting rich is something that is pushed on to people that even kids at a noticeably young age, when asked, say they want to become lawyers and doctors because they want to be rich and have lots of money. Many do not say they want to do it because they want to make a difference in others' lives or find value in that work. They simply know folks who become lawyers and doctors are known to be wealthy and live in mansions. Some young people today even say they want to be YouTubers because they can make money and become rich.

This book focuses on becoming more organized, efficient, and effective with personal finances to pay off debt, save money, and live comfortably. It teaches planning and organization to maintain a healthy financial lifestyle and to build upon what is already there as a middle-class earner.

As the book's author, you probably think I have it all together with my personal finances. The truth is I do fall behind and there are times when I struggle, like everyone else. However, I have the safety nets in place to get back up every time I fall. I am constantly learning to control my spending habits and self-discipline when it comes to spending. Through this book, I am sharing my challenges, vulnerabilities, experiences, and life lessons that have helped me get out of poverty and into financial stability.

Use some of this book's graphs, charts, and visuals to your advantage. Also, use the checklists! They will help you make changes in an organized way. Graphic organizers, like checklists, help us make changes systematically. We must stay consistent and not give up on things we try out after a few times because it is consistency and self-discipline that will lead us to success.

Besides the content in this book, become a lifelong learner of financial success and stability by researching and reading continuously on this topic. We cannot learn everything we need to know from one book. Moreover, we need to learn from different points of view. Whether we take classes, read for research, or ask friends and family, we will grow our knowledge base and improve our money management skills with efficiency and organization!

References

https://www.cbsnews.com/media/7-traits-of-people-who-struggle-financially/

https://www.thesimpledollar.com/save-money/depression-spending-and-bad-money-behaviors/

https://www.psychologytoday.com/us/blog/when-your-adult-child-breaks-your-heart/201612/compulsive-spending-what-you-need-know

https://www.huffpost.com/entry/money-disorder-signs_1_5cba0e5be4b068d795cc389c

https://www.compassion.com/poverty/what-causes-poverty.htm

https://www.theguardian.com/society/2015/jun/30/poverty-negative-spiral-fear-self-loathing

https://www.bls.gov/opub/mlr/2003/04/art2full.pdf

https://www.pexels.com/photo/crop-woman-filling-calendar-for-month-5239919/

https://www.moneycrashers.com/money-saving-benefits-organizing-home/

http://www.moneywisepastor.com/72/importance-organized-financially/

https://60minutefinance.com/10-reasons-people-dont-budget/

https://www.investopedia.com/financial-edge/1109/6-reasons-why-you-need-a-budget.aspx

https://bethebudget.com/why-is-budgeting-important/

https://inspiredbudget.com/

https://www.healthline.com/health/victim-mentality

https://www.franchisedirect.com/top100globalfranchises/rankings

https://www.chase.com/personal/mortgage/education/financing-a-home/what-percentage-income-towards-mortgage#:~:text=The%2028%25%20rule%20states%20that,monthly%20gross%20income%20by%2028%25

https://www.valuepenguin.com/average-household-budget

https://www.upatanangle.com/post/3-major-items-i-cut-from-my-budget-and-don-t-miss

https://www.gracefullittlehoneybee.com/30-easy-ways-reduce-household-expenses/

https://stackyourdollars.com/emergency-fund-examples/

https://www.cnbc.com/2019/05/23/millions-of-americans-are-only-400-away-from-financial-hardship.html

https://www.federalreserve.gov/publications/2020-economic-well-being-of-us-households-in-2019-dealing-with-unexpected-expenses.htm

https://dfpi.ca.gov/wp-content/uploads/sites/337/2019/07/What-You-Need-to-Know-about-payday-loans.pdf

https://www.ncsl.org/research/financial-services-and-commerce/payday-lending-state-statutes.aspx

https://www.experian.com/blogs/ask-experian/credit-education/score-basics/what-affects-your-credit-scores/

https://www.debt.org/credit/improving-your-score/

https://www.fightbills.com/bankruptcy/causes-of-bankruptcy/

https://budgetingcouple.com/cheap-living/

https://www.merriam-webster.com/dictionary/the%20American%20dream

Other titles from Higher Ground Books & Media:

Efficiency and Organization to Achieve More in Life by Ruzanna Hernandez, Ed.D.

Wise Up to Rise Up by Rebecca Benston

The Power of Knowing by Jean Walters

Oasis or Mirage by Terra Kern

Dear You by Derra Nicole Sabo

Breaking the Cycle by Willie Deeanjlo White

Raven Transcending Fear by Terri Kozlowski

Healing in God's Power by Yvonne Green

Chronicles of a Spiritual Journey by Stephen Shepherd

The Real Prison Diaries by Judy Frisby

The Words of My Father by Mark Nemetz

The Bottom of This by Tramaine Hannah

Add these titles to your collection today!

http://www.highergroundbooksandmedia.com

Do you have a story to tell?

Higher Ground Books & Media is an independent Christian-based publisher specializing in stories of triumph! Our purpose is to empower, inspire, and educate through the sharing of personal experiences.

Please visit our website for our submission guidelines.

http://www.highergroundbooksandmedia.com

Made in the USA
Las Vegas, NV
22 November 2022

60065234R00077